A Walk for Jim

Land's End
to
John O'Groats

Sally Thomas

Illustrations by Wilfrid Wood

Published in 2001 by Sally Thomas.

Printed and bound by
Biddles Ltd, King's Lynn, Norfolk

Reprinted 2008

© 2001 Sally Thomas

ISBN 978-0-9558206-0-1

For Jim

Acknowledgements

I would like to thank Berwyn, Michael, David, Daniel and Tamsin for their love and unstinting support throughout the walk and the writing of this book.

My thanks also go to the following: our family and friends, some of whom joined me on the walk and all of whom have proved themselves indispensable in so many ways. Shally and Richard Hunt for their invaluable advice on all aspects of the walk. Colin Inman, Tom Isaacs, my brother Bill Oakes and Shally Hunt for help and advice on the editing of the manuscript. Andrew McCloy and the Long Distance Walkers' Association for information leading to the construction of the route. Nick Brown for his sponsorship and the provision of absolutely essential walking gear. George Michael for his wonderful generosity. Wilfrid Wood for taking on with enthusiasm the design and illustration of this book.

Lastly, my especial thanks go to B&B landladies and landlords throughout the length and breadth of Britain, who by their very existence make journeys such as mine possible; who provide a service that is uniformly first class, and who yet have little idea of the joy with which the sight of their establishment is beheld.

Contents

Introduction	9
Stage 1 Land's End to Cheddar	14
Stage 2 Cheddar to Tarporley	42
Stage 3 Tarporley to Carlisle	74
Stage 4 Carlisle to Kingussie	104
Stage 5 Kingussie to John O' Groats	134
Postscript	166
Lists	170

Introduction

It began with a photograph pinned up on the noticeboard in the leukaemia ward. 'Well done Finlay!' read the caption beneath the picture of an ex-leukaemia patient who had ridden an ancient bike from Land's End to John O'Groats, thereby raising several thousand pounds for leukaemia research. I decided there and then that I too would make this journey, though on foot rather than bicycle. I decided that I would do it whatever the outcome of Jim's illness; if he survived, it would be a thanksgiving, and if not, funds raised would contribute towards research aimed at eliminating this cruel and devastating disease.

Jim, a musician and the second oldest of our four sons, came home from London at the end of November 1997, ashen-faced and ill. We rushed him to hospital and within two days were told that he had acute myeloid leukaemia. The succession of diagnostic tests he had undergone throughout the summer had failed to detect the disease, which was now clearly rampant. This then, was the cause of the extreme tiredness he had been experiencing since the spring.

By a strange quirk of fate, the success he so richly deserved had arrived simultaneously, in the early spring of that year. Jim was a guitarist, singer and songwriter. His own band, Radio Jim, was well known on the London music scene and he played in several other musical groups. But the success he needed on a grander scale had remained elusive until that spring, when a period of intensive song-writing in a new partnership played dividends. One of their songs gained immediate recognition, and on the strength of what promised to be a hit single, the new band, called Trigger, was signed up by George Michael's new record label. Jim was overjoyed. His dream had come true and the future looked rosy; he was working in George's state of the art studio in Highgate, the envy of all his friends and music colleagues - and yet he felt so tired he could scarcely get up in the mornings. He couldn't understand it. But it didn't stop him from continuing to work and carry on with his very active life. The band did a nation-wide tour of radio stations, Jim falling asleep after every interview. Throughout the summer they worked hard, writing new songs for the album. But Jim's health was worsening. In addition to the by now habitual tiredness, he was suffering an extreme thirst and diuresis and by late summer he was diagnosed as having diabetes insipidus. This separate condition, treatable though not curable, proved to be a red herring. We breathed a sigh of relief at the diagnosis, thinking that this was also the cause of his general malaise. But the tiredness got worse rather than better and he was awaiting the results of further tests when he finally drove himself home to Sussex on that November morning.

During his 15 weeks in hospital, Jim displayed extraordinary courage and fortitude. His determination to beat the disease carried him through almost continuous pain, innumerable crises, two courses of chemotherapy, and a period of 28 days when he was without a single white blood cell with which to combat infections. It is no exaggeration to describe leukaemia as a cruel disease. As a blood-borne condition it affects all parts of the body, so that the resolution of a crisis in one organ or part of the body is almost immediately followed by crisis in another. In the end, Jim was literally swamped by the disease, and he died on 13 March 1998. He was 28 years old and it was less than a year after his life had seemed crowned with glory.

We, his family, were left with the knowledge that the unthinkable can occur. As we tried to pick up the pieces of our lives again one thought emerged with some clarity: Jim would have hated to think that our lives were made forever miserable by what had happened to him.

Jim had an enormous number of interests, but there were two that were perennial and about which he was passionate: music and cars. His interest in music was noticeable from a very young age and he appeared to have an innate facility for playing different musical instruments. But the guitar was the love of his life, and throughout his adult years he was rarely seen without one or other of his guitars strapped to some part of his person or luggage. His decision to make music his career was not taken lightly. He knew it would be hard and that there was a good chance he might not succeed. At the same time he felt he had to be true to his ambition and at least make the attempt. He knew he had the talent and musicianship, and it became apparent that he also had the determination and resilience needed in a career characterized by a roller-coaster of hopes and disappointment. Most of all he was a star; he loved people and the limelight and they loved him back.

His passion for cars, bikes, motorbikes, anything on wheels, also derived from his earliest childhood and continued throughout his life. He loved driving and was an addicted spectator of Grand Prix motor racing. It was because of this enthusiasm that from the earliest days of planning the walk, I looked upon it as 'Jim's lap of honour'. I wanted to show him off to the world, and felt somehow that by carrying him with me in my heart, I could do this. There was also a feeling of wanting to compensate him, even in a small way, for all the places and travel that he himself would never experience.

So the reasons for the walk expanded. Having started with the idea of raising money for the Leukaemia Research Fund, it was now becoming a walk to be undertaken in Jim's honour. And as the weeks of planning and practising went by, it became apparent that the walk was going to be of considerable therapeutic benefit to me too, and maybe to the rest of the family. Once the initial incredulity had worn off, my husband Berwyn and our sons were increasingly caught up with the idea of the expedition. They knew how I felt, and indeed the boys had themselves already completed a 350-mile sponsored bicycle ride during the previous summer, also inspired by Well Done Finlay. As Michael, Jim's older brother, pointed out, Jim lives on through his influence on us. Perhaps we all want to catch his valiant spirit and reproduce it in our own lives.

Although I enjoy walking I have never considered myself 'a walker'. Occasional rambles in the surrounding countryside or a walk with friends on the South Downs was about my limit. No walk had ever lasted more than a day. Clearly I was going to have to put in some practice before setting off on a hike that looked like being about a thousand miles. So throughout the preceding winter I tramped around the fields and lanes at home, gradually increasing the weekly mileage but always battling against a lack of time. At the end of one heroic week I had walked 30 miles, but the more usual weekly total was somewhere between 10 and 15 miles. It would have to do. As the departure date drew near, I occasionally filled my brand new backpack with heavy items - potatoes, sugar, tins of cat food - and carried that around too.

Most time-consuming of all during that winter of preparation, was trying to work out precisely how I would get from Land's End to John O'Groats. It suddenly didn't seem so simple and there appeared to be a dearth of information on the subject. I found lots of books on the Coast to Coast Path, the Pennine Way and other long distance walks; even one or two on walking around the coast of Britain. But the only one of use to me: Andrew McCloy's *Land's End to John O'Groats*, was out of print. I finally obtained a copy of this exceedingly useful book, which describes three separate routes, but by that time, after many hours spent pouring over maps and travel books, I had my own route marked out. I wanted the walk to be as direct as possible whilst at the same time being scenic. This was, after all, a chance in a lifetime to see at close quarters a slice of Britain's tremendously diverse countryside. There were particular places that I had often wished to see, such as the Wye Valley, Cromarty, the Quantock hills; others were spur of the moment decisions inspired by a photograph or description in a travel book: the Forest of Bowland in Lancashire, a remote hill in Shropshire called the Long Mynd. Bit by bit the journey took shape, guided by the 'must see' places, helped along by invaluable advice from the Long Distance Walkers' Association and incorporating chunks of Andrew McCloy's western and central routes whenever possible.

In order to convert the distance into manageable proportions I split the journey into five stages. Each stage amounted to roughly 210 miles, giving an estimated total of 1050 miles. I then realised that if I walked 70 miles a week the journey would take me exactly 15 weeks, which was the length of time Jim was in hospital. This was a coincidence too neat to resist, and led to a more detailed planning to ensure that I would arrive in John O'Groats on 26 June precisely.

Last but not least there was the thorny question of what to wear. The pitfalls of being togged up in the wrong gear, or having inadequate footwear, were stressed by all. It seemed that flip-flops would not do. Yet the vast range of walking boots and high-tech outdoor clothing was completely bemusing. Here, I was fortunate indeed to receive invaluable advice from Shally and Richard Hunt[1], who lived locally and were well-known for their 4300 - mile walk around the

---

1. Shally and Richard Hunt walked around Britain's coastline, a journey that took 10 months. Shally's book *The Sea On Our Left*, Summersdale, 1997, is a record of their journey.

entire coast of Britain. Who better to ask? They explained the importance of strong leather boots in insulating the feet from damage when carrying a heavy backpack; they introduced me to the concept of layers of clothing, lightweight shirts, the essential socks. They gave me so many useful tips on every aspect of long-distance walking, that I am forever indebted to them for eliminating the possibility of so many potential disasters. In addition, I had acquired a sponsor in the local firm of Nikwax, who kitted me out in their marvellous range of Paramo breathable clothing systems, as well as promising a generous donation to the Leukaemia Research Fund. Now I was ready and even looked the part!

One thing I was sure of from the start, I wanted to do the walk on my own. In fact, there seemed to be absolutely no point in doing it otherwise. Initially this had caused a flurry of concern. Wouldn't I get lonely? Or lost? Suppose I was accosted, or fell down and broke a leg? With regard to the first two, I had no worries; loneliness was what I wanted, and although I thought it quite likely that I would occasionally get lost, I saw no reason why this should result in calamity with only a short daily mileage to complete. In response to the more serious concerns, I felt that since there was absolutely nothing I could do about either situation, beyond taking reasonable care to prevent their occurrence, I would simply not think about it. I did make one concession though: I would carry a mobile telephone (though not its battery-charger, which would have been much too heavy).

I had decided to start out on the walk on 13 March, the first anniversary of the day Jim died. All the family was coming to walk with me for the first day and I think we all hoped that striding out of Land's End together on Jim's Walk would mitigate to some extent the sadness of the date. Berwyn was going to visit me at roughly three-week intervals along the way, bringing with him the maps and notes I'd left behind in little piles for each stage of the journey. The boys, Michael, David and Daniel, and Michael's wife, Tamsin, were also hoping to meet up with me at some stage of the way. Three and a half months suddenly seemed a very long time to be away from them all. But I knew that nothing that could happen, no hardship, discomfort, fright or loneliness, could ever remotely compare with that experienced by Jim during his illness. The only similarity in our two journeys would be that the duration of both would be 15 weeks.

Stage 1
Land's End to Cheddar

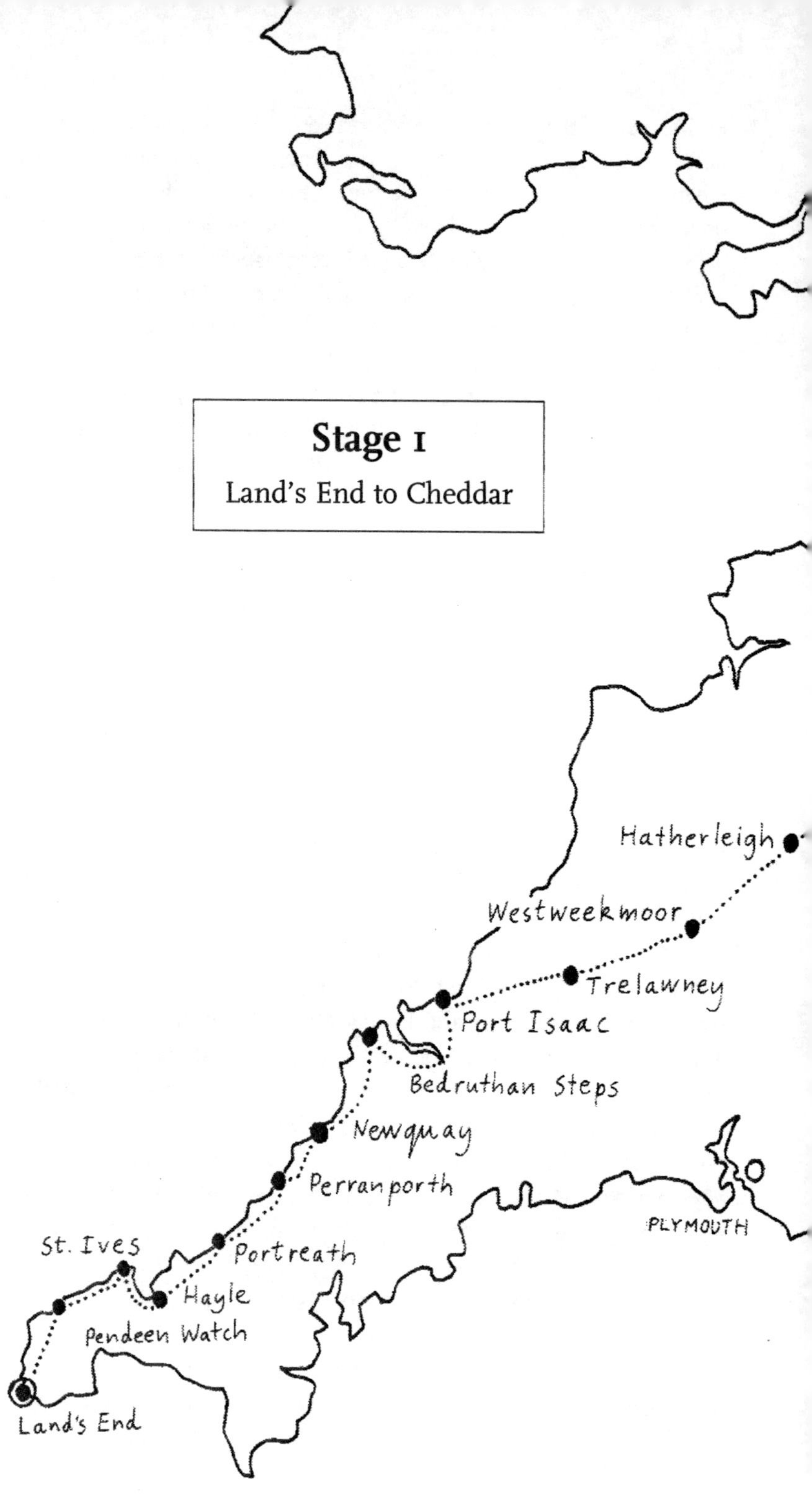

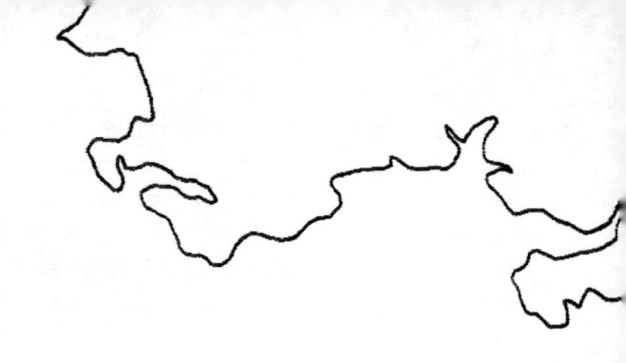

Land's End to Cheddar

SW Coastal Path - N Devon - Quantoch Hills - Somerset Levels
Saturday, 13 March - Saturday, 3 April

OS 203 Penzance

Land's End, *SW Coast Path*. Whitesands Bay, Cape Cornwall, **Pendeen Watch**.	12 miles
Pendeen Watch, Porthmeor Cove, Zennor Head, **St Ives**.	13 miles
St Ives, Porthkidney Sands, **Hayle**.	6 miles
Hayle, The Towans, Godrevy, **Portreath**.	11 miles
Portreath, Porthtowan, St Agnes, **Perranporth**.	12 miles

OS 200 Newquay

Perranporth, Holywell, Fistral Bay, **Newquay**.	11 miles
Newquay, Mawgan Porth, **Bedruthan Steps**.	7 miles
Bedruthan Steps, *leave SW Coast Path*. Tregona, Padstow, Rock, Port Quin, **Port Isaac**.	15 miles

OS 200 + OS 201 Plymouth

Port Isaac, St Teath, Knightsmill, Kenningstock Mill, Tresinney, Watergate, Crowdy Reservoir, Davidstow Woods, Newpark, **Trelawney**.	16 miles

OS 201 + OS 190 Bude

Trelawney, Trewen, Pipers Pool, Gospenheale, Hr. Tredundale, Launceston, Dutson, Nether Bridge, Crossgate, St Giles on the Heath, Tower Hill, **Westweekmoor**.	17 miles

OS 190 + OS 191 Okehampton

Westweekmoor, Germansweek, Eworthy, Broadbury, Northlew, **Hatherleigh**.	12 miles
Hatherleigh, Monkokehampton, Bondleigh, **Zeal Monachorum**.	11 miles
Zeal Monachorum, Down St Mary, Morchard Bishop, **Black Dog**.	8 miles
Black Dog, Puddington, Pennymore, **Tiverton**.	11 miles

OS 181 Minehead

Tiverton, Exe Valley Way, **Bampton**.	8 miles
Bampton, Shillingford, Clayhanger, **Waterrow**.	7 miles
Waterrow, Wiveliscombe, Ford, Pitsford Hill, **Crowcombe Heathfield**.	11 miles

OS 181 + 182 Weston Super-mere

Crowcombe Heathfield, London Farm, W.Bagborough, Park End, Timbercombe, Enmore, Durleigh, **Bridgwater**.	13 miles
Bridgwater, Chedzoy, Stawell, Chilton Polden, **Catcott**.	10 miles
Catcott, Shapwick, Westhay, Wedmore, **Cheddar**.	13 miles

Total	**224 miles**

(20 days walking - average 11.2 miles per day. Days off: 2)

Ruined engine house of a Cornish tin mine on the South West Coastal Path.

Stage I

Saturday 13 March
Land's End - Pendeen Watch

Traffic cones line the approach to Land's End, preventing parking anywhere except within the tarmacked acres surrounding what seems to be more of a theme park, than the pile of rocks I remembered from my youth. Even so, Land's End was deserted when we arrived at 10 o'clock this morning. The Land's End/John O'Groats signpost was nowhere to be seen, and so after drifting around for a while, wondering if there was anything in particular we should be doing on this most auspicious occasion, we finally clustered around the Land's End Hotel and took pictures of ourselves there, just to show that I really did start at the beginning. It was a beautiful sunny day with a keen chilly wind, perfect for walking and a good omen perhaps.

We set off along the South West Coast Path in high spirits, David and Dan both hungry (already)! The boys and Tam careered over the rocks ahead, Berwyn and I following at a more leisurely pace. At one point David led us all down a torturous hillside thickly covered in bramble and bracken, a 'shortcut' that got too steep for Berwyn and me, and resulted in all of us losing the coastal path for an hour or two! On to Sennen Cove and Whitesands Bay where the sea was an incredible aquamarine, quite rough and so crystal clear that even the white froth of the breaking waves was tinged with turquoise.

Every now and then I tried to convince myself that this was it, the start of a walk that was going to last for three and a half months and cover a distance of over a thousand miles. But it was no good - I couldn't really take it in. I felt perfectly relaxed and only the present seemed real: the sea, the Cornish coastline stretching ahead as far as the eye could see, the boys perched on rocky outcrops, picnicking, and all of us together as we lay luxuriously in the warm sunshine.

By mid afternoon we'd reached Cape Cornwall, where we'd left one car, and Berwyn and Tam drove back to pick up the other from

Land's End. Michael, David, Dan and I trudged the last few miles to Pendeen Watch, passing through some old tin-mine workings, all of us getting a bit tired by now. The distance was 10 or 12 miles (the Coast Path book says 12 miles, but my calculations suggested 10) and a most beautiful walk.

We drove on to St Ives where Berwyn and I were booked into a B&B, and later on had a big feast in the town before it was time for the boys and Tam to drive back to Port Isaac[2]. I felt completely desolate on saying goodbye to them. I hadn't thought that it would be so awful.

Sunday 14 March
Pendeen Watch - St Ives

Berwyn drove me to Pendeen Watch and I set off, on my own now! Saying goodbye was a bit chokey but not as bad as it had been last night with the boys. After all, Berwyn and I will meet up again in a few days time, at Bedruthan Steps.

I was in a stupor of tiredness by the time I got here. By my calculations it was at least 13 miles of what the Coast Path guidebook[3] describes as 'strenuous' walking. Up and down, up and down. I think McCloy[4] also describes this section as one of the toughest stretches of the whole South-West Coast Path. Added to that, I got lost twice and once had to go some distance inland before I could pick up the path again. I spent some time skirting a farm because of a furious-looking dog barking at me, only to come face to face with it at the gate on the far side! On closer inspection it turned out to be a spaniel and it was probably quite friendly. Other company on the way was buzzards, kestrels, sheep, and maybe a dozen or so other walkers. Lovers on the points, gazing out to sea.

Finally arrived in St Ives at about 6 o'clock. The last stretch seemed never-ending and I was thankful that at least I hadn't had to carry my pack. Lavender oil to feet and supper in room.

2. Our holiday cottage.
3. *Walk The Cornish Coastal Path*, by John Mason. HarperCollins, 1998.
4. Andrew McCloy. His book, *Land's End to John O'Groats: a choice of footpaths for walking the length of Britain*, provided invaluable information on the navigation of large sections of the route.

Monday 15 March
St Ives - Hayle
Felt fine this morning and set off in bright sunshine for what was going to be a much shorter day. But this was the first day I'd had to carry my backpack and I realised immediately that the big disadvantage of warm weather is that if you're not wearing it, you have to carry it, and the combined weight of both fleece and anorak seemed considerable. St Ives to Lelant was quite pleasant, along the coast next to the little branch railway, and then it was mostly road walking to Hayle, quite hard on the feet. The RSPB own the head of the estuary and it's famous for its waders. I only saw masses of seagulls and a couple of oyster-catchers. Wrong time of year I expect. Got to Hayle at midday, starving hungry despite the big breakfast, and bought a large cheese and vegetable pasty, which I ate sitting in the sun on a bench by the harbour.

Because I was so early I contemplated going on to Gwithian, which looked to be the next place of any size, but the guide-book makes no mention of B&Bs there, and since it's another six miles after that to Portreath I decided not to risk it. Good thing too, I began to feel more and more exhausted as I plodded up and down Hayle looking for accommodation. Nowhere. The one place I was directed to was closed. The pub did B&B but, amazingly, was fully booked until April. Just as I was thinking I'd have to get the train back to St Ives, which is awash with accommodation, I came for the second time to this great hotel, the White Hart. This time I didn't give a thought to the possible expense and booked myself in. It's £29.50, but worth it just this once and at this stage of the journey it's surely prophylactic. I've been in bed most of the afternoon and have used all the teas and sugars. I've soaked myself for hours in a deep bath in my own private bathroom and surveyed my scratched and swollen legs. The scratches are from fighting my way through the gorse yesterday when I got lost. My face is all puffy too and I'm not feeling too good. It's not surprising I suppose, yesterday was exhausting and the day before that was a bit harrowing.

So rest is necessary, and I've been cheering myself up by writing screeds in my notebook about Gangan[5] and the old days. I was

---

5. My maternal grandmother, who lived for many years in Amersham, Bucks.

reminded of her this morning as I walked through the quiet of St Ives, and smelt that soft indefinable smell that so often wafts through suburban streets: flowers, damp earth, hedge, grass, tarmac, rubbish - impossible to isolate all the ingredients. Or to recall the smell unless you're there.

Something good happened when I first got here though, even if it did upset me. I'd felt a bit miserable and so was lying on the bed thinking to have a little sleep. But just as I was about to doze off, I saw Jim, as clear as anything. I saw him exactly as he was, before he got ill, but the time scale was the present. He was standing at the corner of two fields, on the footpath and looking at my map in its polythene cover. He was turning it around the other way up, as if he thought it was upside-down and laughing because he couldn't puzzle out where we were! Big brown eyes wide, eyebrows raised, like he did. It was only for a second and then I woke up, although I didn't think I'd been asleep. It was precious and lovely, but also made me cry.

Tuesday 16 March
Hayle - The Towans - Godrevy - Portreath
White-boy groover - the best! That's what Michelle[6] said about Jim in the memory book. It was the music that put me in mind of Michelle's remark, when I was sitting in the local hostelry, eating an enormous plateful of steak and ale pie, chips and four different vegetables, the whole lot doused in thick gravy. Jim would have loved it. I think the music they were playing was dance music, I'm not sure, but in my mind's eye I could just see him as he must so often have been, dancing in a pub or club, long lean body going absolutely with the music. What a beautiful boy! No wonder they all loved him so. Not out to show off or impress (though if it did impress I'm sure he'd be wise to it) just dancing for the pleasure of it.

I left the pub rather abruptly and walked around the harbour, here in Portreath. The sky was crystal clear and Orion was up there, shining on his shoulders and his feet. My shoulders are shining too, quite painful today. Feet are fine though.

---

6. One of Jim's friends. The memory book was a book of blank pages left out for people to write in on the day of the funeral.

Earlier on, before I pictured Jimmy dancing, I was thinking that this is really something to relish. Here I am, all on my own, in a pub 'of an evening', in this remote little Cornish village. Never been here before and probably I'll never be here again. It feels like I'm a shadow, flitting into town, hovering a while and gone in the morning. Clint Eastwood, without the cloak and without the intentions. Nobody knows me and nobody cares. At this stage in my life it's very restful.

Wednesday 17 March
Portreath - Porthtowan - Perranporth

Exhausted, can hardly write. I'm in a nice B&B though, and have just eaten the sandwiches I bought in the town earlier.

This morning I abandoned the Coastal Path for the first part of the journey and went inland as far as Porthtowan. This was to avoid a hazardous stretch of coastal path described in the guide book as being 'narrow' and where care must be taken because the Ministry of Defence boundary fence is situated close to the cliff edge. No-way José. So I went inland instead, walking for several miles along the 'tramroad' as suggested by my landlady. This was a leafy walk where the old trams to the mines used to go, and it was very pleasant and flat and shady.

Rejoined the coastal path at Porthtowan, and followed it from there to Perranporth, a further eight miles off. The views of the Cornish coastline were spectacular but there were whole sections of the path when I couldn't look anywhere at all, it was so terrifyingly steep and close to the edge. Making it worse, and actually quite dangerous I think, was the ground underfoot which was shale, or scree and sometimes stuff from old mine workings, so loose and crumbly that my boots slipped and slithered all over the place. Conscious of the sheer drop yawning down to the rocks far below, just inches from where I had to walk, I crept along with my eyes glued to the path just in front of my feet, whispering 'Courage!' to myself like Little Grey Rabbit. My stomach was turning over and several times I felt I couldn't go on any further, except that the only alternative was to go back the way I'd come. How on earth do mountaineers and rock climbers do it? Do they have no imagination at all when it comes to picturing your own body slipping and hurtling down onto the rocks below?

I also kept thinking of Jim and how he kept his head above water despite his desperate situation, and my worries paled into insignificance. This was something I'd thought about during the planning stage of the walk at home, how I'd only have to think about how much he endured, to put fright and misery into perspective. Funnily enough though, I'd never anticipated this particular problem: my dislike of heights. I'd imagined I would need to think of his courage when it came to general exhaustion, or when confronted by dogs, or men or broken feet - but I forgot all about vertigo! At any rate, I absolutely hated that stretch of the coastal path and was never more pleased to see anywhere in my life than Perranporth when it finally hove into view. Sorry I didn't appreciate the scenery.

The day was hot too, despite the sea mist, and so my pack was heavy with all my outer clothing. Threw away my powder compact and the Nikwax[7] leaflet - desperate measures!

Thursday 18 March
Perranporth - Newquay

Slept for nearly 10 hours last night and felt fine this morning. I set off across the sands to Newquay, no more perilous cliff edges and a dramatic change in the weather - cold and windy for the first time.

Walking all along the sands this morning was exhilarating, though quite hard work battling against a fierce northerly wind. Hat, gloves, scarf on for the first time. Perran Sands are indeed beautiful and I had them to myself. The Army is in possession of the stretch of headland at the far end, and two soldiers were watching from the cliff-top beside one of their big black net climbing frames as I struggled up the sand dunes. I hoped I wasn't trespassing on Ministry of Defence territory and it seemed OK as they didn't shoot me. I gradually made my way up to the headland, taking care not to touch any military debris, which could blow up and kill me, so the notices said. Saw a stoat for the first time ever, quite close-to on the headland bordering the Army property. When I reached the northern side of the headland at Holywell, the wind was so strong I had to literally hold on to the posts so as not to be blown over.

---

7. Nikwax. Manufacturers of weather-proofing materials and Paramo Breathable Clothing Systems. Their headquarters are situated in Wadhurst.

Holding my woolly hat on with one hand, and Stick[8] in the other, I descended with difficulty and gave heartfelt thanks that at least the wind was blowing me inland rather than seawards.

After Holywell I turned inland in order to cross the River Gannel, and was quite glad to get out of the wind. From then on it was quiet Cornish lanes all the way to Newquay, or rather, Porth, just the other side of Newquay where I'd booked a B&B. I arrived in a bit of a heap and was dismayed to find the house all shut up. I hung around for an hour or so until the landlady returned to find me sitting on her wall writing postcards. It was worth the wait though because this is a bargain B&B: £11 a night, shower in the room and TV as well! The bed's a bit lumpy and hard but I'm so tired it really doesn't matter. As I get tougher I dare say I'll be off dancing and sightseeing when I get to a place, whereas now all I can think of is hot water and bed (only one place so far has had a bath, but a shower is OK too).

Every day there seems to be a different part of me in trouble. Yesterday it was the back of my right thigh, the day before that shoulders. Today it was toes, so I've oiled them and rubbed my feet on the wooden thing Tam gave me. So far, however bad I feel by the end of the day's walk, everything is recovered by morning.

During the last two days I've been thinking that as the journey is going to take 15 weeks to match the length of time Jim was in hospital, I should write down some of the stages of his illness. Though I've written snatches of thought in another notebook at home, I haven't been able to write about that time yet. Perhaps starting at the beginning would be a good way to do it. Would Jim have wanted me to write of it I wonder? He probably wouldn't care one way or the other. But some record of what he went through would demonstrate his courage, greatness of heart and mind, and sheer physical strength.

Saturday was the day I set off from Land's End and it was a Saturday when Jim drove himself home from London. He arrived while Berwyn and I were having lunch, and he looked absolutely terrible, with a pallor I'd never seen before. We hadn't expected him home and so I rushed off up the drive to greet him, and as I gave

---

8. My walking stick, handcrafted by Chris Velten, was made of blackthorn with a yew handle, the tip made of ram's horn..

him a big hug he stopped me because his shoulder hurt so badly. 'I think I'm dying', he said, to illustrate how awful the pain was. He'd had the most appalling journey, stopping several times because he felt so ill and the pain in his shoulder was so bad. He'd been feeling terrible the day before and James[9] had offered to drive him home but Jim wouldn't hear of it.

We called the emergency doctor, who arrived quite quickly and was concerned and completely nonplussed. He rang the hospital to say he was sending them someone who he thought needed a physician, but maybe a surgeon. At any rate he needed to be there, and pretty quickly. Berwyn and I took him in and Berwyn was in such a state of anxiety that he dropped us off at the wrong door, where the A&E had been some ten years before. Jim was admitted to a fairly slack-looking A&E and was seen by the doctor. By this time the pain in his shoulder was easing a bit but his throat was getting sore. We had arrived at the A&E by about 3pm but it was 7pm before he was admitted to a ward. By the time he got to the ward his throat was agony and we were all feeling a bit desperate.

The next two days, Sunday and Monday were days in limbo. Blood tests failed to be analysed because the blood kept clotting in the test tube. The reason for this became clear later when the diagnosis showed that his platelets were also affected by the leukaemia. At the time it was very frustrating. Jim got worse and his sore throat continued to be agonizing ('life-changing' was how he described the pain of it in the diary he kept for a while) however much they gave him in the way of painkillers and the analgesic throat-wash that he had specifically requested. The ward was busy and under-staffed but Jim was well able to look after himself, demonstrating even then that he was going to be in charge of what happened to him.

By Tuesday morning his condition had worsened so much that he was moved up the ward to the place opposite the nurses' desk. He was switched from the care of the physician to the haematologist. He had a roaring gut infection also by this time, and said the pain in his bum was as bad as the pain in his throat. Other patients also had the infection and the ward was pronounced closed. By late

---

9. James Jackman. A friend of Jim's who, with Jim and Arianne, formed their successful band, Trigger

Tuesday afternoon the results of the last lot of blood tests finally came through and Berwyn was told that Jim had acute myeloid leukaemia. The curtains were around Jim's bed and I was with him, he was in a terrible state, sore throat, diarrhoea and feeling awful. Berwyn came in and told us the news: 'It's acute myeloid leukaemia.' I grabbed Jim into my arms, but he pushed me off because I was hurting his shoulder and all the rest of his painful chest and abdomen. I said, 'There's been a mistake,' but Berwyn said 'No.' Jim, recovering from the pain of my hug, opened his eyes wide and said to me 'That's what your Dad had wasn't it?' I hastened to reassure him that things had moved on a lot since those days, how leukaemia was no longer considered such a serious disease, people were cured of it all the time and so on. Jim told us later that hearing he had leukaemia was nothing compared with the relief of being given a dose of Valium. All he wanted was to be knocked out for a bit - a respite.

Then at last things started to happen. He was moved to the Intensive Care Unit for the night where he received high quality nursing care. Everything was put in motion for him to start chemotherapy as soon as possible. During the time that he was being got ready to go upstairs to the ICU I went into the corridor and looked out through the window at the car park. That car park we were to get to know so well over the next three and a half months. It had started to snow, just a few flakes. I'll never, ever forget that time. Thinking about it now, I suppose what I felt was stricken, but the most vivid thing about that memory is those big white slowly-falling snowflakes. Later on we saw Jim settled in the ICU and looking quite cheerful. Spick and span and overall relieved that at last something was happening and people were taking things like his sore throat seriously. Berwyn and I went home and Berwyn had to tell people the news.

The next day he came back to the ward, but now to a side ward in the haematology corridor. At least he had his own room now. Everything was got ready and the following day, Thursday, he started his first ten days of chemotherapy. The medical and nursing staff prepared him for the worst but, as he said, it couldn't make him feel any worse than he already did. And so it was; he was never sick and only a bit nauseous. But he became much more ill, and I think this was also the time when his voice started to go and swallowing became difficult.

The nights were the worst, he said - no sleep. The staff didn't want to give him more analgesics or sedatives, but he was getting tired and rightly felt that he needed a good nights sleep. We spoke to the medical staff, but it was weeks before that side of his care was sorted - that only came with the advent of the 'pain nurse' from the anaesthetic department, and from her to the Macmillan sister.

Throughout all this time Jim had been having daily blood tests and constant transfusions of blood and platelets. The chemotherapy also had to be given intravenously through his arm - because of his clotting problems it was too dangerous to insert a central line through the chest wall. So imagine what all this was like for a boy who throughout his life had had a horror of needles, hated the sight of blood, hated even the sight of an engorged vein. And as his veins got used up, it became more and more difficult to put up a new drip and they'd have to 'dig' for a vein. It was truly pitiful.

Friday 19 March
Newquay - Bedruthan Steps

This section of the cliff path was easy going, the weather was balmy and I thoroughly enjoyed this, my last day on the South West Coast Path. Probably because there are more walkers in this area there was quite often what I dubbed a 'ninny's path' - a second track a few feet further in from the cliff-edge. Excellent! I met two friendly American girls who were full of admiration for what I was doing, when I explained where exactly John O'Groats was! In fact, they said, I really should be on the radio. Their husbands were stationed at the Air Force base nearby at St Mawgan. I also met my first backpacker, a New Zealand girl on a week's holiday from London. We beamed at each other, kindred spirits on the Coastal Path, and compared notes about rucksacks and route and what the going was like, specialized stuff like that! I've been quite surprised by how few people there are walking, up till now. I suppose it's too early in the year.

Best thing was the knowledge that Berwyn was going to be there at the end of today's trek. We'd arranged to meet at Bedruthan Steps and he was already there when I arrived at 2pm precisely. He'd been looking for some steps, not realizing that the place is called after the gigantic 'step' rock formation spaced along the beach! It was so good to see him. We drove home to Port Isaac where I shed my boots and had a long wallow in a hot bath. Steak for supper and all lovely.

Saturday 20 March
Bedruthan Steps - Port Isaac
Berwyn delivered me back to Bedruthan Steps in the morning and I set off in carefree manner, carrying only my day pack full of sandwiches.

I said goodbye to the Coast Path, and walked inland through the quiet network of narrow winding lanes and occasional footpaths to Padstow. The countryside appeared to be hosting quite a lot of Saturday morning leisure activity, biking, kite flying and even some parachute jumping out of little aeroplanes that landed in a field nearby. From Padstow I took the ferry to Rock. The weather changed, becoming cold and blustery, and I had a chilly picnic lunch sheltering under a rock on the beach. More lanes and footpaths to St Minver and Port Quin, from where I fair skipped across the fields to Port Isaac. Getting there, slithering down Postman's Walk and seeing our little house across the harbour, was just wonderful.

It was a longer journey than I had expected. My pedometer said 17 miles but the map wheelie measured 15. The business of measuring the daily mileage is not as precise as I would have wished. Today I could have had three different totals if I included the mileage as totted up from road signposts as well! Obviously these are not exact, but I'm beginning to think my pedometer isn't either. I think I'll rely only on the map wheelie from now on. My calculations for this part of the journey were a bit rushed as I'd left the planning of this stage of the walk to the end, and then ran out of time. Scotland is even less precise. Although I know exactly where I'll be going I haven't yet divided up that part of the route into separate day's walks. But that's a long way off.

Sunday 21 March
Day Off; Port Isaac
Lovely day off! Breakfast in bed and big lunch at Port Gaverne. My appetite is enormous. I'd expected to be losing weight with all the strenuous exercise, but if anything I think I've put on weight! Feet quite good though, except for painful little toes on both feet. Rash, bruises, swellings all subsiding. It rained for the first time since I left but of course it didn't matter a bit. Stove going, boiling hot.

Monday 22 March
Port Isaac - The Rising Sun, Trelawney
Another day without pack because Berwyn met me at Trelawney and brought me back to sleep here. Tomorrow will be the same. It does help, not having to carry all that weight.

Quiet lanes to St Teath were followed by a nasty mile on the A39. The landscape then changed quite dramatically, becoming more and more remote with tiny lanes and rippling streams. As I approached Bodmin Moor and Roughtor it got higher and wilder, the lanes so narrow that if a car had come by I'd have had to do a quick scramble up the steep bank. Then a long straight wind-blown road led across the moor to Crowdy Reservoir, where I had my picnic lunch gazing across at the rocky summit of Roughtor. The only activity was sheep-related: the occasional landrover bouncing by, sheepdogs in the back, tongues lolling, and the expert herding of a huge flock of sheep in the distance. On through Davidstow Woods, which was stuffed full of Christmas trees and great piles of tyres, and then into the airstrip (this is part of a McCloy route). The last leg of the journey was a rural idyll over Davidstow Moor, where wild ponies, sheep and cattle grazed the common agricultural ground, and then more lanes, farms, fields and intermittent views leading to Trelawney and *The Rising Sun* - where Berwyn and I missed each other! I'd forgotten that I'd marked two maps with slightly different routes, and we each had one. He'd set off to meet me along the other route! All well in the end though and we were back home before the rain started.

One more cosy night here after this and then I'm on my own. This is a lovely little interlude, knowing where I'm going to sleep each night, being cosseted, cooked for and chauffeured back and forth to the next day's starting point.

Tuesday 23 March
Trelawney - Westweekmoor

Longest day so far: 17 miles and legs nearly falling off by the end of it.

The morning's walk was perfect, deep in the hidden lanes by the River Inny, and through Pipers Pool to more hilly, remote and grassy-centred lanes, reaching almost to the outskirts of Launceston. By lunchtime I'd crossed the border into Devon and sat to eat my picnic on the banks of the River Tamar. I must have sat too long, because when I tried to get up, my legs gave way under me - I literally couldn't stand for a few moments! Gradually the strength returned, but I hobbled with bent knees for quite a while. I'd arranged to meet Berwyn at Westweekmoor and the last few miles of road seemed interminable. I was about an hour late and Berwyn was getting worried because the place didn't figure on his map at all, nor was it marked on any signpost. He was making enquiries inside the little school when I finally I got there and we were both very relieved to see each other. Drove back to Port Isaac for the last time.

Wednesday 24 March
Westweekmoor - Hatherleigh

Really didn't want to leave Port Isaac and then felt miserable saying goodbye to Berwyn at Westweekmoor. In a way it feels as if this is the real start of the walk, because up till now I've been cushioned by the proximity to Port Isaac and even more by having Berwyn around. Next time I see him will be in Hereford.

Today was quite hard going, but better than I expected given the state of my legs and toes after yesterdays long haul. Once Berwyn and I had parted, I began to feel OK again surprisingly quickly. The walk was through quite mixed countryside, high moors and scrub giving way to little lanes and agricultural land.

Got to Hatherleigh in good time and the B&B that Berwyn had booked for me yesterday is great. The Acorns is an old, low-ceilinged, beamy tea-room which also serves as the cyber-cafe for North Devon. A brand new computer sits resplendent in the little booth in the middle of the café, in place of the ancient till and flowery aprons that you'd expect to see there. It was installed by the

County Council, for the use of the local inhabitants, and my landlady tells me that theirs was the only establishment that would have anything to do with the enterprise. They're a very nice couple, made quite a fuss of me and wanted to hear all about the walk. Another couple staying here gave me my first donation of £5 for Leukaemia Research. They had come all the way from Norfolk to attend the big auction sale that took place yesterday in the Market Place. Berwyn went to it when he was finding the B&B and said it was the most amazing sale he'd ever seen. Everything you could think of was being sold there: food, furniture, livestock, eggs of every colour and description, and a huge collection of sporting equipment and memorabilia, which is what the couple from Norfolk had travelled to see.

Thursday 25 March
Hatherleigh - Zeal Monochorum

Easier journey, not so hilly, but raining. I stopped to deck myself out in all the wet-weather stuff for the first time and it worked very well. It was misty too, so I couldn't see Dartmoor, which was just a short distance away. The Devonshire countryside is so easy on the eye though, with its peaceful lanes, gentle hills and quiet, quiet, quiet. During the course of the day I must have seen every conceivable type of farm animal, including those rarely seen on farms nowadays, such as turkeys, old breeds of poultry, donkeys, even a cart-horse, as well as those you'd never expect to see on a farm until a few years ago: deer, ostriches and guinea fowl. But mostly there were cows, breathing steamily in the damp air. Lovely, smelly, muddy cows, hundreds of them. Overall, the smells were a mixture of primroses and muck-spreading, a truly lovely combination. Buzzards continue to circle overhead and I've learnt to recognize their lonely haunting cry.

Garden birds began to be more in evidence as I neared Zeal Monochorum, and when I arrived in this pretty village, the only sounds I could hear were birdsong and a tractor rumbling away in the distance. I sat on a bench outside the church to await Alison[10] who'd arranged to meet me here, and sure enough, after about ten

---

10. Alison Wraith. We met as student nurses at the Middlesex Hospital in London, 1960.

minutes the village peace was briefly shattered by the arrival of her little Ka whizzing round the corner, and the happy squeakings of two old nurses meeting again after a gap of some years! She whisked me away to a grand historic old inn, the other side of the A30 at South Zeal, all previously booked, and luxurious finishing touches (bath salts and champagne) brought by Alison. It was such a treat to see her again and we ate hugely and chatted until we were hoarse, much as we used to do in the old days.

Friday 26 March
Zeal Monochorum - Black Dog
Said goodbye to Alison back in Zeal Monochorum (Monk's Cell) and then it was a mere seven-mile hop to Black Dog. I sauntered along the lanes and through the picturesque village of Down St Mary, now all bathed in warm sunshine. Everywhere looked fresh and sparkling after the rain. Hedgerows still wintry, but gathering themselves to burst into their spring abundance. Already there are primroses and the white starry flowers that I think are called Star of Bethlehem, plus all the daffodils that people have planted along the tops of walls and banks. The lanes are a delight to walk along and it hardly occurs to you that there might be any traffic. It reminds me of the countryside of my childhood.

I'm in an incredibly tidy and beautifully kept B&B. Everything is painstakingly prepared, alive with knick-knacks and little bowls of potpourri. Matching curtains, wallpaper and duvet covers. Ducks on the walls and around the bath-tub, wooden butterflies and exotic sea shells bursting with bath oil capsules. I really should have taken off my boots!

Today was fun and I think I'm beginning to get into the swing of all this.

Saturday 27 March
Black Dog - Tiverton
Got another donation (£5) from my landlady. She was sweet and had tears in her eyes when she asked how old Jim was. Maybe her son is that age. The beautiful house was built by her husband and her son, everything top quality and lavish. Oak doors and gold taps. The glass in the dining room where I had my stately breakfast was

amazing, all crystal and crinkle and with a theme of ducks as in upstairs. She's lived in Black Dog all her life and admits that 'it is quiet here.' Understatement of the year.

From Black Dog (the derivative of this wonderful name seems to have been lost) it was a quick march through more lanes into Tiverton. Got there about 2 o'clock and visited the Tourist Information Centre to book the next two nights. They could only fix me up for tomorrow though, as the day after that I'll be out of their area. Later on met Vawa[11] and Paddy at the B&B Vawa had booked for me from home ages ago. It was the very first B&B to be booked, and I remember thinking that it was quite a landmark in the planning of the walk. It was so good to see them both and we had a big meal out in the local Italian restaurant.

Sunday 28 March
Tiverton - Bampton

Vawa and I breezed along the eight miles of the Exe Valley Walk and arrived in Bampton at 1pm. We met up with Paddy at *The Seahorse* and then they left for Port Isaac. Next time I see them will be after about 1000 miles later, at the end of June!

Bampton is a lovely old town, big river running through it (not the Exe) and some very handsome buildings. I'm in one of them now, in a big four-poster bed, and I have the house all to myself because the proprietors have gone out. It's very snug and cosy and I've no doubt that I'll sleep solidly the whole night through. This is something new for me, the world's worst sleeper during the last year or so. Since the start of the walk I've been sleeping for at least nine hours every night, without ever waking up. It's brilliant and I'm wondering if athletes and footballers sleep like this all the time?

I still haven't found a place for tomorrow night so I'll leave early and trust to luck.

---

[11]. Vawa, my sister, is only rarely called by her real name of Valerie. Paddy is my brother in law, and his real name is Adam.

Monday 29 March
Bampton - Waterrow

Didn't get all the way to Wiveliscombe. I was so completely drenched by the pouring rain that when I reached Waterrow and saw this nice-looking pub advertising good accommodation and home-cooked food I was in there like a shot. And yes, they had a room. 'In fact,' he said, maybe because I was dripping pools of water onto the floor and generally looking like a drowned rat, 'you can have the Flat!'

So here I am, ensconced in the ground floor flat of a pretty little house opposite the pub. Outside the garden is full of flowers and even has a river running through it. I've made myself at home and spread my sopping wet clothes all over the sitting room. I hope they'll be dry by tomorrow.

Whilst I'm walking, so many thoughts burst through my head - about Jim and all sorts of other things as well. But by the time I've reached my destination and am shored up in my room, all I seem to have the energy for is a quick factual record of the day's events. This will make for very boring reading later on but it can't be helped. Live in the present - that's the thing. After all, living each day as it comes is something I've got used to during the past months, and is probably why I've had no difficulty acclimatising myself to the walk mentally. I remember years ago reading somebody's advice to anyone undertaking a long walk, which was never to think beyond the day ahead, (or the next 10 miles, can't remember which). Easy for me, it wouldn't occur to me to do anything else, so taken up am I over where I'm going to today (especially when I haven't got a B&B booked).

Tuesday 30 March
Waterrow - Crowcombe Heathfield

Poured with rain most of the day, and I went the wrong way for the last bit which added a couple of miles to the journey. Got to the youth hostel here shortly before 3pm and there was a notice on the door saying it was closed until 5pm, but that the Wet Weather classroom and toilet in the grounds was open.

And that is where I have been for the last one and three-quarter hours. When I arrived I was soaked to the skin on my top half and so changed into my only other shirt. My fleece and anorak are hanging up in the entrance to the classroom and have made quite a puddle on the floor. Luckily my bottom half keeps beautifully dry in the Paramo trousers. I've eaten the pepperoni I had in my pack and written lots of postcards. But it is cold in here and I feel quite chilly. About half an hour ago a car drew up and two people went into the back entrance of the YH. So after a bit I went and knocked, then hammered on the front door, but nobody answered. They feel they must keep to the rules I suppose, and 5 o'clock is when they open and so that is when they'll open. I know they're aware of my presence though, because they could see me through the classroom windows when they drove by. I've brought some milk and bread with me, and the leaflet says there is a small shop inside, so hopefully I'll be able to make supper for myself. This place is miles from anywhere, and I'm too wet to be able to go out anyway.

Despite the rain, the day's walk was good (except the last bit when I went wrong and was milling about in a maze of tree-lined roads for what seemed like an eternity). Through the mist and drizzle the fields and low hills looked cosy and enclosed. I suppose it's fortunate that I actually like rainy days in the country. I'm in Somerset now, though I'm not sure at exactly what point I crossed the border. It's different from both Devon and Cornwall. Cornwall is unique I think, so variable, wild in parts, ugly sometimes, but with an appeal all of its own. Devon is a county I hardly knew and it's incredibly beautiful, and lonesome too with its traffic-free lanes and remote farms and villages, and hardly a day when I didn't have buzzards crying and circling overhead. Here in Somerset it's different again, the gently undulating countryside and tidy affluence reminds me of Sussex (probably Somerset is more affluent than both Devon and Cornwall put together). The soil is a deep reddish brown and the houses are built of a distinctive warm sandstone the same colour. The hedges are out more here too, and I saw violets and the first cow parsley, and literally tons of primroses. Larks, wrens, robins and my first yellow-hammer have replaced the buzzards. People are very friendly; they want to show me the way all the time.

Saw two dead badgers in the lane. One of them had a printed card next to it saying: DO NOT TOUCH THIS ANIMAL. IT MIGHT HAVE TB. This must be part of all the controversy over whether or not badgers are spreading TB to dairy herds.

5pm. I can go in now!

Wednesday 31 March
Day off; Crowcombe Heathfield

Last night I had a strange dream about Jim in which he was in hospital with leukaemia but against all expectations was getting better. This first part of the dream was quite detailed and realistic, but it ended with a complete change of scene. He and I were outside on a grassy slope, Jim aged about three years old, golden curls gleaming in the sun, laughing and happy and I knew he'd recovered from the leukaemia. He was running around, pushing a little wheelbarrow in which there was a box. The box was a bird's nest, and there were some little birds inside. I was hovering by, watching him and hugging him every now and then, picking a splodge of mud off his cheek. He was laughing and so was I - couldn't believe it, he was well again after all. Then I woke up and that was awful.

This is my second day off and I was so pleased I'd organised to have it here, especially after such an unpromising start. The Quantock Hills were one of my central 'must-see' places, like the Long Mynd and the Forest of Bowland; places that I'd decided my route had to go through. I think the Quantocks appealed mainly because of the name, plus their proximity to Exmoor and Lorna Doone country (which was too far out of my way).

It came up to all expectations. I went in the little train, Western Somerset Railways, from Crowcombe Heathfield station, two minutes walk away from the youth hostel, to Watchet, a journey of about half an hour. It was an excellent way of seeing the area, and I thought the Quantock Hills as seen through a train window were beautiful, as were the isolated farmed acres nestling in the slopes lower down. Watchet was a bit messy and run-down in the centre, but the old part of the town had some beautiful old buildings and the beach had everything - stones, seaweed, sand and lots of rock pools, plus quite a big harbour around the corner. I had a sumptuous lunch in the Bridge Hotel - four pieces of fried fish with four different sauces on a bed of salad and chips. It came with crusty bread and butter, which I promptly put away in my rucksack for the YH supper and breakfast. After lunch I trundled down to the beach again and stretched out and even slept a while until it was time to take the train back. The weather was better, quite sunny, and I felt refreshed. My next whole day off will be in Church Stretton, Shropshire.

Thursday 1 April
Crowcombe Heathfield - Bridgwater

Well! I'm glad to be out of that youth hostel! It was a fairly miserable place, but maybe that was the unfortunate first impressions lingering on. I had an eight-bedded dormitory all to myself the first night, and only one other person the second night. It was self-catering, so there was a big kitchen, but the fridge didn't work and they had an exceedingly sparse selection of provisions. You could hardly call it by the name 'shop'. The only other people there were a family busy with their kids and one other couple. TV lounge but no TV. I'd run out of book so I pinched one from their bookcase and read on my bunk each evening.

My feet were really hurting today, little toes especially. The actual mileage wasn't huge, about 13 miles, but the first six were steeply uphill all the way as I went over the Quantocks, and then downhill all the way for the last seven. Walking downhill puts quite a strain on the toes, but even so I prefer that to climbing uphill.

It was the most strenuous day's walk for some time and I felt tired when I arrived, but am recovering well in this beautiful B&B with thick carpets, tea-making facilities and a bathroom down the corridor *with bath!* Once again the decor is lavish, not frills 'n' shells this time, but Homes and Gardens, matching wallpapers and freezes, pine furniture and chintzy bedspreads. Posh china and huge plants. Everything in pristine condition and what the estate agents would call 'well-appointed'. Bridgwater Tourist Information got me this B&B, which I must have passed on my way in (adding another mile or two to the journey). It's a bit expensive - £22, but never mind for once. Accommodation seems to be more expensive round here, and I hadn't the strength to go wandering around and knocking on doors to find a cheaper place.

Plus of course, I've just had two nights in Colditz - time for a bit of luxury! Bridgwater is not very nice, and absolutely full of people, with kids on school holidays jamming up the shopping centre. I saw some truly awful eating places when I was looking for lunch.

This morning, when I was on top of the Quantocks, I saw my first swallow and heard, but didn't see, a loud rackety woodpecker boring holes in the tree right above my head. It was so close, but though I peered up into the tree from every angle I couldn't see it, even with the binoculars.

Tomorrow it will be flat, all across the Somerset Levels to Catcott, something entirely different. Somerset is such an extremely varied county.

Out of touch completely with the news for the last two days, so now I'm going to have an evening with the telly. The news is awful of course - bombing of Kosova.

Spotlight has given way to *News West*. Local news is always very interesting, adds a new dimension and gives you a feel of the place.

Friday 2 April
Bridgwater - Catcott

I've been looking forward to the Somerset Levels. It wasn't one of the central must-see places like the Quantocks, because up until the time of planning the walk I'd never heard of them. But I'd thought it would be a refreshing change after all the hills of the West country - plus, I liked the sound of all that water, even if it was going to be in the form of 'drains'. And I was right. It was a change, but more than that - I really loved it. The sky was enormous, bland and grey ahead of me, banked up with clouds behind. Clearly it was going to pour with rain but even that didn't stop me from thinking, 'This is just what I like.' In fact, it was a stronger feeling than that. I felt the place exactly matched my mood. Narrow, straight lanes, lonely and yet domesticated. Nobody about at all, again like the countryside of my childhood. Gates into fields that lead nowhere other than the fields you could see. No surprises, no hidden agendas. A few trees lining the ditches here and there and that was all. In the distance a tractor was ploughing the deep red earth over the only hill. Quiet, reflective, restful. I thought it was magical. It was so still I hardly expected any birds even, and jumped out of my skin when a pair of mallards flew out from the stream at my feet. There were several pairs of ducks and a heron, but except for a single lark overhead, that was the only wild life I saw.

I used to like wild places, and felt invigorated by them. But I'm not drawn to them anymore or feel I have a need for wild and vigorous settings. The wild has requirements, makes demands. Even the sea requires something of you to match its glory, whether serene or exuberant. The Somerset Levels are flat, they require no physical exertion (a definite plus) or mental exertion (it's all *there*, like an open book) or emotional exertion - it just quietly reflects how I feel. It just is.

During the early part of the day I could still hear the distant rumbling of the M5 that I'd crossed over just outside Bridgwater. But the noise was behind me, and the black and increasingly menacing clouds were also behind me. And I wondered, a bit fancifully, whether this flat, calm open country ahead will be like my life from now on? The traffic was past, and even if the clouds caught up with me, well, they'd only bring rain and I could cope with that.

Saturday 3 April
Catcott - Cheddar

More Levels, though some of them not so attractive, encompassing a huge peat works at Westhay, and some very derelict farming near Catcott. A huddle of dejected cattle stood in a filthy cramped yard and a lot of bony, dirty horses were grazing the scrubby grass in a field nearby. Further on, a small flock of really manky sheep were being driven down the lane by an unsavoury looking character. I stopped to let them overtake me and my smiles of greeting elicited no response whatsoever. The man was assisted by a nervous-looking boy, pale and thin and as pathetic as the rest of the live-stock.

I got to thinking that Somerset is the home of the Great Communicators. If you stop to ask the way, the directions given are mind-bogglingly long and detailed. People go out of their way to help you, and one man literally went out of his way at least a mile to show me how best to get to the bridge over the M5. Most remarkable of all was the sheer number of notices affixed to houses and gates: 'Welcome to our Hearth,' 'Cat lover lives here,' 'Please don't let the dog out. Thank you,' 'Mind the dog,' 'Beware of the dog.' Sometimes the message was communicated by the picture of a large dog and a caption below telling you how many miles per second it was able to accelerate between the house and the gate. There was hardly a house that didn't confide in you. But today I saw my best notice yet. This was a board tacked onto a field gate that proclaimed in large letters: NO WATER BIRDS. I spent some time gazing at it and for the life of me couldn't see who the information was directed at!

Arrived in Cheddar about 4pm and so had an hour to kill before the youth hostel opened. Had tea in a very swish little café and looked around the town. The hostel is quite good, central heating and cooked supper. The people are funny though, no, not funny, wrong word. That's the problem. They're such a dour lot. Both the people running the show and the people staying there. The one thing they seem to have in common is a zilch sense of humour. Anyway, slept well in my top bunk and was very comfortable.

End of Stage One. One fifth completed already! I feel I shall reach the end of the journey almost too soon at this rate.

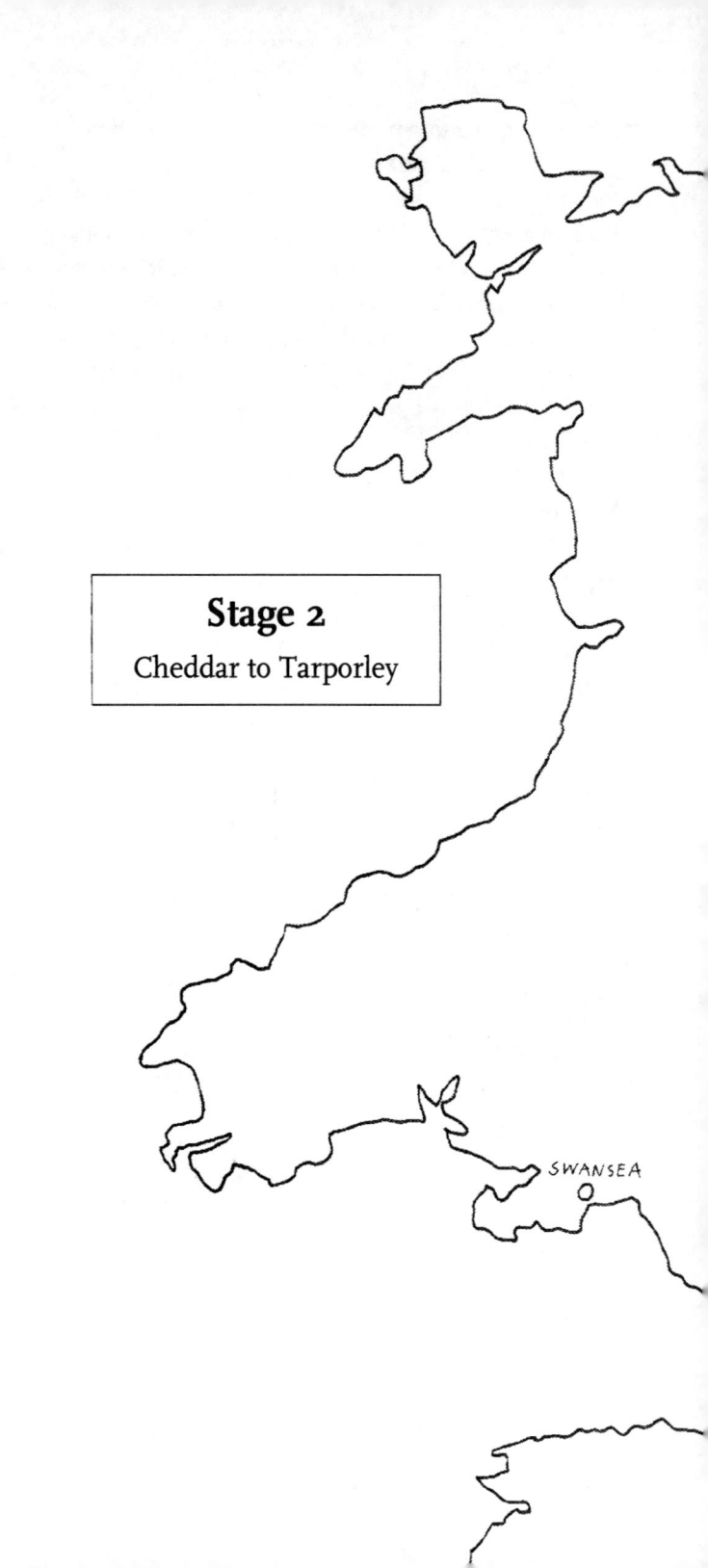

Stage 2
Cheddar to Tarporley

SWANSEA

○ LIVERPOOL

● Tarporley

● Whitchurch

● Wem

● Shrewsbury

● Church Stretton   ○ BIRMINGHAM

● Clun

● Knighton

● Kington

● Bredwardine

● Kenchester

● Hereford

● Ross on Wye

● Welsh Bicknor

● Monmouth

● St. Briavels

○ ONDDA

● Tintern Abbey

● Chepstow

● Pilning

○ BRISTOL

● Portishead

● Churchill

◉ Cheddar

Cheddar to Tarporley

Severn Bridge - Wye Valley - Offa's Dyke - Long Mynd
Sunday, 4 April - Friday, 23 April

OS 182 + 172 Bristol

Cheddar, Lower Farm, Black Down, Rowberrow, Dolebury Warren, **Churchill**.	9 miles
Churchill, Sandford, *Cheddar Valley Railway Walk*, Yatton, Clevedon, **Portishead**.	18 miles
Portishead, Sheepway, M5 Avonmouth Bridge, *Severn Way* to **Pilning**.	13 miles
Pilning, *Severn Way* to Severn Bridge, **Chepstow**.	8 miles

OS 162 Gloucester

Chepstow, *Wye Valley Walk*, **Tintern Abbey**.	5 miles
Tintern Abbey, Bigsweir, **St Briavels**.	5 miles
St Briavels, Whitebrook, Redbrook, **Monmouth**.	9 miles
Monmouth, Symonds Yat, **Welsh Bicknor**.	9 miles
Welsh Bicknor, Kerne Bridge, **Ross on Wye**.	8 miles

OS 162 + 149 Hereford

Ross on Wye, How Caple, Capler Wood, Mordiford, **Hereford**.	16 miles

OS 148 Presteigne

Hereford, Upper Breinton, Sugwas Pool, **Kenchester**.	7 miles
Kenchester, Byford, Monnington Walk, **Bredwardine**, leave *Wye Valley Walk*.	7 miles
Bredwardine, Upper Castleton Farm, Whitney toll bridge, Brilley Mountain, R.Arrow, Upp. & Lr. Hergest, **Kington**.	13 miles

OS 137 Ludlow

Kington, *Offa's Dyke Path*, **Knighton**.	14 miles
Knighton, Offa's Dyke Path to Garbetts Hall, *leave ODP*, Upper Treverward, *Jack Mytton Way* to **Clun**.	8 miles
Clun, Clunton, *Jack Mytton Way*, Plowden, Long Mynd, **Church Stretton**.	16 miles

OS 137 + 126 Shrewsbury

Church Stretton, Carding Mill Valley & *Shropshire Way* to **Shrewsbury**.	14 miles
Shrewsbury, Uffington, *Shropshire Way* to Grinshill, Clive, Tilley, **Wem**.	14 miles

OS 126 + 117 Chester

Wem, *Shropshire Way* to Creamore Bank, Whixall, Alkington, **Whitchurch**.	10 miles
Whitchurch, Grindley Brook, *Sandstone Trail* to Bulkeley, Peckforton, Beeston Castle, Wharton's Lock, **Tarporley**.	16 miles

Total	**219 miles**

(20 days walking, average 11 miles per day. Days off: 0)

Waymarks and stiles along the English/Welsh border.

Stage II

Sunday 4 April
Cheddar - Churchill
On my way by 9.30 am. Saw Cheddar Gorge from the path above it, very impressive. I got a bit lost afterwards, adding a few miles to the day's journey. Easy walk across part of the West Mendip Way and then through a wooded plantation to Churchill. There was a lot of mist so I couldn't see Lakes Chew and Blagdon. I did see the perfect circle of Cheddar Reservoir though, from the tops. Easter holidaymakers everywhere sitting outside pubs, drinking in the sunshine (both meanings).

B&B news: I've just had a bath in the most amazing bathroom you could ever imagine, especially in the respectable quiet of suburban Somerset! It's all shades of pink and puce with a lush purple carpet. The puce walls are interspersed with panels of scrolled and decorated frosted glass and more huge painted mirrors and puce panels surround the enormous (puce) sunken bath. It's the biggest bath I've ever seen and would hold a family of four with no difficulty. The rest of the house seemed quite normal.

This evening I walked about a mile from my B&B on the main road to the phone box in Churchill, a pretty little village, smothered in magnolia blossom. The effect of so many trees growing together in such a small tucked-away place was stunning. I shan't ever forget Magnolia Churchill and its glorious puce bathroom on the highroad!

Monday 5 April
Churchill - Portishead
Too far. Feel awful. Legs and feet and toes on fire. The rash has come back - from the socks I think, or the heat. It was quite a hot day so the pack was heavy. Got here about 5.30pm, so that's about eight hours walking and half an hour for lunch (chips from the fish and chip shop in Clevedon which I ate on the beach). It was Easter Monday bank holiday so Clevedon was packed out, as was Portishead.

Except for Clevedon, all parts of the walk were good, through flat, pleasant countryside. From Churchill, I went across the fields to get to the Cheddar Railway Walk, which takes off at Sandford and followed it to Yatton. Walked the lanes from there as far as Clevedon. Re-crossed the M5. From Clevedon the coastal path to Portishead twisted up and down, in and out on the coastline, with good views of the Avon estuary. But I was so tired by then - and hot, and having to ration myself with water. At one point when I thought I must be nearly there, a woman sitting on a bench told me it was another four miles to Portishead! I couldn't believe it, but she was right. Portishead, when I finally reached it, was huge and sprawling and it took me ages to find my B&B, the Dockmaster's House, which I'd booked ages ago from home. Just as well too, I didn't see any B&Bs at all on my way here, and my landlord says there are altogether only six B&B beds in the whole of Portishead, four of which are here in his house. The reason it took me so long to find it was because it's in a fairly remote part of the town, right on the Avon estuary, and as you'd expect from the name, huge ships travelling to and from the docks are passing by right outside my window. Trouble is I've no energy to appreciate it. Want to get up and have a look but legs won't let me. It's a lovely B&B though, top quality and very comfortable. In addition to the free boat show outside.

Jim had infinitely more to put up with than anything I'm going to suffer. I've been thinking about him a lot today, it seems to go in phases like it did in the early days. Perhaps I'm regressing. And all the dreams I'm having, most of the details of which I can't remember.

Tuesday 6 April
Portishead - Pilning

Yesterday was 18 miles minimum, probably quite a bit more if I was to count all the to-ings and fro-ings when I got lost on the footpaths going to Sandford. But I'm trying not to exaggerate the mileage in any way, so I've recorded 18. It was the hardest day so far and I felt really terrible yesterday evening. Alright again this morning after nine hours solid sleep, except that my ankles are still covered in the rash and during the day today it became apparent that I was getting my first real blister.

Today has had several markers, 1) crossed the border into the county of South Gloucester, just after Avonmouth, 2) walked across a *footbridge* going over the M5 which was a bit nerve-racking, and 3) walked along the side of the M5 motorway to cross the Avonmouth bridge. This last wasn't very pleasant, especially if you haven't got a head for heights. Also it was very windy, coming in great gusts, so I kept as close to the car lane as possible. There was an awful stink coming from about a hundred portaloos stationed every few yards along the bridge, presumably for the use of the workmen doing repair work on the other side of the motorway. I wonder where it all goes?

The bridge was a mile long and at the other end I was immediately engulfed in a vast complex of main roads, motorways, huge extended roundabouts and HGVs thundering along to the docks and industrial sites lining the roads. Bristol is just down the road. I had a little carbohydrate picnic of Lucozade and Danish pastry in a park in Avonmouth village, an oasis in a sea of transport and commerce. Then it was a fairly straightforward walk, at first on the A203 and then along the estuary following the Severn Way path. Walked underneath the new Severn Bridge and here at my B&B in Pilning I look out onto the approach road to it. Definitely a day of bridges.

It's a good thing the mileage wasn't very big today. First thing I did on arriving here in this very comfortable farmhouse B&B was to wallow in a gorgeous bath and examine my blister. It's about half an inch diameter on my left heel and very painful. I really appreciated the long soak in the bath here, especially after last night's fiasco in Portishead. After that awful long day all I'd wanted was to have a quick hot shower before collapsing on the bed, but the water was freezing cold! It remained cold no matter how long I ran it and so I had a miserable shower. In the morning it turned out that I hadn't pulled the cord to switch on the power! Berwyn would say 'typical!'

Farmers in this area had a raw deal when compensation money was being assessed over the value of land taken over by the new Severn Bridge. It was prime agricultural land but not recognized as such by government officials. It's still not sorted, after all these years. My landlady and her husband (and their son who also works on the farm) have lost millions, and they are now thinking of moving to Wales. They're a real old farming family, and so friendly and concerned. Edith insists I send her a postcard from John O'Groats - if I get there! She's quite worried I'll fall by the wayside I think!

Dave Gray[12] arrived here at about 7 pm. He had booked himself into a B&B just along the lane, arranged for him by my landlady. It was lovely to see him and we went off in his car (bliss!) for a pub supper. I feel quite touched that he should have come all this way to join me for just for a few hours walk. We arranged to meet at 9.30am.for tomorrow's walk over the Severn Bridge to Chepstow.

Wednesday 7 April
Pilning - Chepstow

Dave and I set off for the Severn Bridge crossing, me hobbling slightly from the painful blister on my heel. We got to the Severn Bridge quite quickly and had a great walk over, it actually BOUNCES when you jump on it! It wasn't as queasy-making as yesterday's Avonmouth M5 bridge either, probably because the path is wider. We could see for miles, and the elegant new bridge strung high across the water further down the estuary looked magnificent and yet somehow frail silhouetted against such an immensity of sky. It was very impressive, and has to be one of the high points of the walk so far (not magical like the Somerset levels though).

We got to Chepstow and found a B&B for me, and a taxi to take Dave back to Pilning, and thence home to London. He was such a sweet fellow and such good company. After he'd gone I had a long rest in my bedroom over the bar of the *Coach and Horses* to try and cure my heel, which is still very painful. Later on I rang James[13] as arranged, as he and Arianne[14] are coming for the day tomorrow. James gave me the astounding news that George Michael is donating £10,000 to Leukaemia Research Fund in response to my letter. I was completely gob-smacked! I'd been thinking he might give me about £500, which, added to the Nikwax £500 would make the nice round sum of £1000. I think it's a magnificent thing for him to do.

12. Originally a friend of Michael's, now a friend of all the family and a Biker for the LRF.
13. James Jackman. Jim's friend, songwriter and keyboard player for Trigger.
14. Arianne Schreiber. Jim's friend, singer and joint songwriter for Trigger.

Jim always said he was a good bloke and that he did a lot to help charities and so on. He would have been proud and pleased by this I know. For some reason it has made me feel quite upset as well though. All this money, and all so insignificant in comparison with a life. Jim's life. I don't know how we bear it.

Local news: *Wales Today*

Thursday 8 April
Chepstow - Tintern

Arianne and James arrived at my bed and breakfast inn at midday. They'd set their alarm clocks for 7am and James was immensely impressed with himself for having woken up before it went off! It was great to see them, they came in like a breath of fresh air, all beaming and smiling and Arianne's hair done up in its fantastic blue and red fibre-optic ribbons. I felt quite proud in the pub that they'd come to meet me, fuddy-duddy middle-aged walker!

So we set off to try and find the Wye Valley Walk[15]. Not as easy as I thought and we seemed to be walking alongside the racecourse long after we should have left it far behind. James quite quickly distinguished himself as a born-again Rambler, and after several mistakes by me, he was elected Our Leader and given the map. It was a very picturesque walk, all woods and ivy-clad trees with glimpses of the river here and there. Arianne was in her element - such a romantic!

It was lovely for me to have them. They were telling me about Jim and how much they and all the friends and fellow musicians talk about him. James says he finds it easier to talk about him now. He told me about how hard it had been to carry on with the music writing, feeling as though he'd lost an arm and a leg. He said nobody had ever inspired him as Jim had. Also how much he'd appreciated the total honesty they had with each other in their work. Socially as well, they described how Jim was the central being in all their lives. As Michelle said in the Memories book, Jim was the common denominator of all the different groups of friends.

---

15. *Walking Down The Wye*, by David Hunter. A Cicerone Guide, 1992.

I love being with Jim's friends. I love to hear them talk about him with such affection and admiration. Sometimes with our own friends, I feel the need to tell them how special he was, and it never seems to come out right. It always sounds like the adulation of a grieving mother. With Jim's friends I don't need to say anything, they know what he was like and it's so good to hear them talk.

We got very muddy. Arianne's lovely orange trainers copped it worst of all but she didn't care. James had on the navy blue trainers that Jim had persuaded him to buy, a pair like his own, comfortable and such good value. James insisted on carrying my pack all the way, which was great for my blistered foot. We got to Tintern Abbey about 5 o'clock and after a cup of tea James shared a taxi with a couple of Americans to get back to Chepstow and pick up Arianne's car. She and I meandered in and out of the Abbey ruins, taking lots of photos. She was as entranced by the Abbey as she had been with the ivy-covered trees, and is determined to come back one day to use the place as a 'photo opportunity!'

I'd booked myself a rather expensive B&B before I left Chepstow, and thank goodness we had the car in which to find it, because we circled round the place for ages before finally locating it high up in the forested hills above Tintern. We had a big meal at the George Hotel later on. James and I had two meals for the price of one and Arianne had all her veges and rice and salad. Over supper we discussed everything from Jim to the war in Yugoslavia, God and the Quakers, the payment of Rabbis, the music business, and back again to Jim. They are such a sweet thoughtful pair and I had a lovely day. They left for London at about 10pm, complete with my letter for George to thank him for his magnificent donation. Apparently he'd been very touched by my letter and impressed about the walk, and had even toyed with the idea of joining us today! James was also amazed at the sum promised, but said how often they talk about Jim, and how much George had liked him and rated him highly as a music colleague. Unquestionably, Jim's influence carries on.

The mobile telephone finally gave up on its batteries, completely dead now. Only had time for a quick phone call to Berwyn. Forgot to say Happy Anniversary as per usual!

Friday 9 April
Tintern - St Briavels
Followed the Offa's Dyke Path along the River Wye from Tintern to Bigsweir because it keeps to the river-bank, rather than going up in the hills which the Wye Valley Walk does at this stage. The three miles from Brockweir to Bigsweir were probably the most beautiful miles of the walk so far. The day was bright and blue, the going easy and the scenery quite magnificent. I made a mental resolution to bring Berwyn here, maybe in the autumn when the colours would be even more glorious. In this early springtime the colours are muted, delicate greys and greens forming a sandwich between the separate blues of the sky and river. I took lots of pictures, Stick masquerading as a foreground figure. Lots of ducks in loving pairs and once in a group of four swimming nose to tail in perfect synchrony, as if joined by an invisible thread. Bird song all the way. Flat short grass to walk on so you don't have to keep looking down to make sure you're not going to trip over a rock or step in some dog-shit. It was perfect.

At the tiny picturesque village of Bigsweir, I left the river and heaved up the two miles sheer hillside to St Briavels where my B&B was booked. That was hard going because it was so steep and the weather was very hot. Found the B&B, a tiny cottage, very pretty but smelling rather doggy, and quite unlike the pristine-clean, sparkling B&Bs I'd encountered up till then. I'd booked this one weeks ago from home. It was recommended by the youth hostel that had been already fully booked, and was actually cheaper than the YH, so my little old landlady informed me! She must have been at least 80 and told me she'd been doing B&B for 37 years. She and her husband used to run a B&B for the actors and actresses at the Old Vic in Bristol. She was very sweet, widowed now, and very much on the ball. Two other people called to ask about B&B, but having seen the room they went off again saying they'd let her know. 'They'll not come back,' she said, and sure enough they didn't!

Had a pub supper with the locals and made the mistake of saying how quiet it was here. 'Oh no! It's not usually like this..... You should see it sometimes' etc.! The implication that it was sometimes a veritable whirlwind of metropolitan activity I found hard to believe. It must be one of the quietest places I've ever been to in my life. Even quieter than Black Dog. No movement of any kind, no traffic and not a soul to be seen except the two or three locals in the pub. My landlady had recommended that I go to the Crown for my supper, the pub for local people and 'travellers', whereas the posher one, the George, was for 'tourists'. I felt quite pleased by the distinction. I was a traveller, not a tourist!

This is England again (Gloucestershire). Back to Wales again (Monmouth), in the morning.

Saturday 10 April
St Briavels - Monmouth

After the steep descent from St Briavels (and a detour of half a mile on a footpath that should have cut off a mile but instead brought me back to where I'd started) it was more, gentle, idyllic river walking along the banks of the Wye. Whitebrook, Redbrook, and then on to Momnouth.

I've seen five dead lambs in the last two days, plus several that just don't seem well, hardly bothering to jump up and follow mum when I come along. One lamb was lying so still as I drew close, its mum was frantic - stamping her feet at me and desperate for the lamb to get up and follow her. But though I thought I saw the lamb's ear twitch once, I think actually it was dead. All these dead lambs seem untouched, not bleeding or hurt in any way, as if they might have been attacked by a fox or a dog. And they were not tiny new-borns either.

Back on the Wye Valley Walk. Crossed and re-crossed the Wye in and out of Wales. Monmouth is the birthplace of Henry V and Mr Rolls of Rolls Royce. It's a busy town, friendly, historic and with two big rivers, the Wye and the Monrow.

Tomorrow I'll see Davy and Little Dan![16] I do miss Berwyn and the boys. I had long chats on the phone to Mikey and Tam who are at home this weekend, Mikey doing up his much loved old Audi ready to sell it. They're going to take over my Clio. Hopefully I'll have my new car when I get back - otherwise my walking will have to continue!

Local TV news: *Midlands Today.*

---

16. Davy, Little Dan, Mikey: family nick names. Jim was also called Jim-a-long by me, and Jimmy by his friends.

Sunday 11 April
Monmouth - Welsh Bicknor

Quick walk to Symonds Yat to wait for the boys at the Saracens Head meeting place. They arrived promptly at 1pm looking so dashing and sweet and grinning from ear to ear! I was so excited at seeing them, and I think they felt it had been a long time too. It's four weeks and a day since we all walked out of Land's End. I felt quite forcibly that the sight of their beaming faces as they rounded the corner of the building is one of the pictures that will remain with me forever, one of the abiding memories of the walk. We had a lovely day. I heard all the news and they both looked well and happy. They took it in turns to carry my pack when we walked up to Yat Rock after lunch. Dan had forgotten all the things he was supposed to be bringing me - telephone battery charger, letters, photos! Left them all at Mamgu's[17] where they stayed last night.

Their bike ride to France is May 22nd. This is their second cycling expedition and it's so good to think of them all going off again, not sponsored this time of course - just doing it for fun, and for Jim. Last year's cycle ride in aid of the Leukaemia Research Fund, raised nearly £7000, a fantastic amount considering it was all from friends and relatives and local people.

David and Dan are very funny together, it reminded me of the holiday in the Shetlands when it was just those two and they were such fun. They brought me a carrier-bagful of presents: bath-cubes, sweeties, little packs of Rollos, a ball, a yoyo, and a gaudy little child's umbrella, all of which will come in very useful I'm sure!

We talked a bit about the walk and my reasons for doing it. It's good to know they're completely in accord with the whole project and so supportive, especially as it does affect them. Their world has been torn apart as much as mine by what happened to Jim, their grief equal to my grief. The four of them were always good friends, their lives closely intertwined; they shared many interests and increasingly, as they grew older, many of the same friends. They are so young to come face to face with such loss; Michael had his thirtieth birthday just three days before Jim died; David was 26 and Dan only 23. And even though they are big grown up boys, living away

---

17. Mamgu. Welsh for grandmother. Berwyn's mother.

from home, the fact remains that I'm more or less unavailable to them for these months.

The reasons for the walk were quite simple really, but powerfully compelling, so that from the start I knew I'd never give up the idea, and that it would take an event of mammoth proportions to prevent me from completing it. The initial idea for the walk was of course to raise money for the Leukaemia Research Fund, cribbing the idea from the ex-leukaemia patient who had been in Jim's ward. But I soon realised that it was much more than that - I wanted, and still want, to do it for Jim himself, to go on doing things for him. And it's also reciprocal, because of the influence that he continues to have on our lives. Although the walk is the sort of thing I've often vaguely wanted to do, I'd never have done it without this happening to Jim. Then, there was the feeling of somehow wanting to try and make up to him for the loss of a lifetime's experience. One of the harshest truths to accept has been that he of all people, so exuberantly fond of life and appreciative of new experiences, has had it cut so miserably short. I suppose I feel that by carrying him with me in my heart, on what I think of as his lap of honour, I can at least show him some of the things.

For myself, I always knew I would enjoy the walk but it wasn't until I actually started off that its therapeutic benefits became apparent. It clarified in my mind the other day when I was trying to explain it to someone: 'It's an interlude', I said, and knew immediately that that was the truth of it. No big deal. No 'finding myself' or 'being free' or 'working things out'. Just an interlude. A little walk every day, listening to the birds and looking at the varying countryside, and thinking about Jim quite a lot. Just one day after another and still being Clint Eastwood really. It's become quite normal.

It's odd that people do sometimes have a problem with understanding why I'm doing it - except for the cast-iron fund-raising aspect of course. No problem with that. It's when I try to explain the more nebulous reasons that a bemused look comes into their eyes and I know I've lost them. The fault lies more in my poor delivery of the explanation, through awkwardness, embarrassment, lack of clarity, than in their understanding. People are invariably sympathetic, and always want to go along with you and your ideas, however peculiar. I suppose it's a question of my not knowing how to wrap up and present thoughts that originate more from the heart than the head. Usually I don't bother, but sometimes I try to explain it, mainly because I feel undeserving of the 'doing-good' accolade, which is entirely inappropriate in my case. Basically I'm doing the walk for selfish reasons, and though I'm not averse to making money for the LRF, I think that its main purpose as far as I'm concerned is to make the walk a more socially acceptable enterprise.

Anyway, the boys know exactly what it's all about, and so do all the family and that's the important thing. We had such a happy time and I have to say it was with rather a heavy heart that I watched them out of sight as they went back down the path to Symonds Yat. I continued on my Wye way, as far as Welsh Bicknor where I was booked in at the youth hostel. A quite good hot supper was followed by a failed attempt to watch Corrers[18], because although there is a TV here, it's on the blink.

I gave back the book I stole from the Crowcombe Heathfield YH, and since the reading material on display here consists entirely of educational and nature magazines, some schoolchild will get a nice surprise to discover this somewhat raunchy novel snuggled in amongst the National Geographics!

Monday 12 April
Welsh Bicknor - Ross on Wye

The Welsh Bicknor youth hostel was the best I'd stayed in so far, friendly warden and well-run. It was beautifully situated, on the banks of the Wye and completely isolated. In the night it was fearfully wild, the wind howling in the great trees just outside and rattling the windows of the hostel. Because I'd arrived via the river path it felt as if I was miles from anywhere, and it was quite eerie on my own in the eight-bedded dormitory. There were only five of us in the whole 46-bed hostel, and it was quite a sizeable building with a chapel in the garden. This morning I realised that it wasn't as cut off as I'd supposed; there is a village, Goodrich, about a mile away, and there were houses on the opposite bank of the Wye further along.

I kept to the river path as far as Kerne Bridge, where Goodrich Castle looms above high up on the hillside. It looked magical, like

---

18. Coronation Street. I have been an addict for many years.

in a fairy story. The river-banks and woods were entirely carpeted with bluebells and wood anemones and the light was brilliant with intermittent sunshine piercing through massive dark clouds. Sadly, my camera appeared to have finished off its reel of 24 photos (bought yesterday in Symmonds Yat) and I had no spare film. So no photos of Goodrich Castle, which is one of the most splendid sights I've seen.

After Kerne Bridge I abandoned the Wye Valley Walk for small roads going more directly to Ross on Wye. This was mainly because of a very sore blister on my right little toe. Toe blisters are made worse by walking downhill and so I thought it prudent not to go uphill either. Got to Ross by early afternoon and found a good B&B near the river. Went off hot foot, lippity-loppity not very fast, to get food and do some washing in the launderette. David had remembered to bring me some Nikwax LOFT so I was able to wash all my outer water-repellent garments.

Since then I've been nursing my feet here in the B&B in preparation for a bigger day tomorrow. I've decided to walk all the 15 miles to Hereford rather than stop in Mordiford, so that I can have an easy seven-mile day when Berwyn gets here on Wednesday.

Tuesday 13 April
Ross on Wye - Hereford

Today was a day to remember! Whereas yesterday was a day of gentle manners, ending in domesticity, today was wild, worrying and exhilarating. It's a tragedy that I have no photographic record of it, because the camera has I think gone phut again. I gave it one last chance when I was walking through some fields above a bend in the river when the sun was shining on the new pale yellow shoots of corn. It would have been a most arty shot, with the big curve in the river below, which looked quite dramatic today, the yellow cornfield and a long view of dark purpley hills in the distance against a black sky. It was superb. But the camera has definitely given up. Never mind, the picture is there in my mind, probably more so than if I'd been able to 'snap it.'

Within 20 minutes of leaving Ross, the weather that had been forecast was upon me. I'd started off in brilliant sunshine, the sky a vivid blue and not a cloud in sight. But in no time at all thick layers of midnight clouds appeared on the horizon ahead, smiling. You were warned, they said! A strong north wind was blowing and I hurried in the face of it to a line of trees, aiming to get there before the heavens opened. And I did, but because thunderstorms had also been forecast, I didn't dally in their shade after all and had gone another 100 yards before the storm finally burst over my head. I madly began to unpack my waterproof gear, and as I did so all the postcards I'd written yesterday evening fell out of my pocket and flew across the ploughed field. I retrieved them all eventually and put up the little umbrella the boys gave me to protect me from the onslaught. But as I struggled again to get all the mackintosh stuff out, little umbrella held between my knees, a great gust of storm force wind whisked it away - and for the second time I was sprinting across the ploughed field, this time chasing after the gaily dancing, bobbing little umbrella! Eventually I was duly kitted out in all the water-repellent paraphernalia, whereupon the squall ceased as quickly as it had begun. It got very cold then and for the first time I was really glad of my warm Paramo fleece and outer gear. In fact my clothes were perfect, because although I did get wet, the sun shone between the squally showers of hail and rain and dried me out.

For the first few miles I felt hugely relieved that even though the weather was so stormy and wild, at least my toe wasn't painful. Also, I was finding my way on the Wye Valley Walk, which was now all across fields, and therefore less easy to find than the previous few days of following the river. I was (foolishly) relying purely on the long-distance path way-marks, so that if I did lose the signs I'd have no idea where I was on the map either. I really didn't want to risk ambling around the Herefordshire countryside with at least 15 miles to go. But here was another comforting thought - at least in Hereford there would be a bed for me, even if I got there late, and so the spectre of sleeping in the silver bag[19] didn't raise its head! Even so, every now and then I had the horrors when I lost the way-marks, and thought, 'well! That's it!' Altogether, the walk was brilliant, the clouds, the light and shade, the stretches when I wasn't sure whether or not I'd missed the path, followed by oh joy of joys,

---

19. A survival bag made of lightweight tinfoil, for use in emergencies.

there it was - the little round sign with the leaping salmon appearing again like a beacon to carry me on to the next stage of gradually increasing worry or despair!

All this time my little toe was getting much worse and long before the last stretch was in sight I was hobbling painfully. It's odd how the intensity of pain fluctuates, sometimes almost disappearing and then suddenly returning with a vengeance, regardless of terrain, up or down. It was definitely worse downhill though, and so once again I abandoned some of the path from How Caple to Mordiford and kept to the less switchback route of little lanes. It was very hilly nonetheless and the views of the surrounding country were splendiferous, better than Symonds Yat.

I heard the first cuckoo of the year and the bluebell woods are in full bloom. Spring has definitely arrived, despite the icy wind and great blocks of hail. The squalls of hail continued throughout the day, and with each shower the wind became terrific. I had a job to walk straight. Around midday I sat on a stile under a yew tree to have a rather spartan lunch - flapjack, cheese portions and water. It was very cold so I didn't hang about. Rejoined the Wye Valley Walk at Mordiford, having passed through some idyllic lanes and hamlets.

The last stretch began between the two rivers of the Wye and the Lugg. It was a battle to walk here too because the footpath went along a raised causeway, built to manage flooding of the two rivers, and therefore completely exposed to the elements. There were literally hundreds of sheep and lambs. Despite being in Herefordshire for the last two days I've seen no Hereford cattle. Plenty of Friesians, but no gentle, square, white-faced Herefords. Is this because of BSE I wonder?

In Hereford at last, I plodded round the entire city trying to find the Tourist Information Centre. I've realised (too late to be of use today) that I must ignore most of the signs when arriving in a strange town because they're directed at cars, and so take you all around the outskirts of the town and via the municipal car parks. I walked six times the distance I needed to have done. The TIC was right there in the city centre. I got there eventually and they found me a B&B not too far away. Phoned Berwyn who is in Wales and will be here tomorrow. Can't wait!

I had an unexpectedly posh meal. The first place I came to was Cafe Uno, so I went in and had a delicious pasta dish and two glasses of wine. Wished I'd put on my evening scarf! It's interesting in a strange town, just passing through. I find I use the time quite intensively and I'm always curious as to how people live in different places. Suffused with wine, I struck up a conversation with the waitress, who was most attentive and friendly and not very busy at that time of the evening. I asked her where she felt she lived, in relation to the UK: Midlands or the West? 'Midlands!' she said, with a vehemence that surprised me. I'd asked the question because I'd been interested to see the local TV news called 'Midlands Today' even though Hereford is so far west. But for my waitress friend, 'West' meant 'Wales', and she certainly didn't consider that she belonged there, even though that was where she was born. 'By the way,' she said, out of the blue, 'Do you know about the dead people?' She proceeded to tell me about the dozen or so skeletons found under Church Street, near the Cathedral, people who had died, or been killed, during the plague. She was fascinated by it all and would have made an excellent tourist guide.

Wednesday 14 April
Hereford - Kenchester

Despite yesterday evening's exhaustion and limping gait, I was completely recovered by this morning. And Berwyn arriving soon after breakfast was the icing on the cake! It's three weeks since we saw each other, and talking on the phone is not the same at all. He'd spent last night in Wales, which is why he got here so early, but had woken up to deep snow this morning! So my weather of yesterday was matched by snowstorms across the mountains into Wales.

We caught up with each other only briefly then because I had to walk the seven miles to Kenchester. We arranged to meet at the church there (having established there was one) and Berwyn walked in to Hereford to sightsee and take my camera to be mended if possible. We met at 1pm outside the church as planned and I sat back luxuriously in the car as we drove off to find somewhere for lunch and then to stay. Berwyn's idea was to book us in at Kington, two days walk ahead, and then he could have two nights and me three, all in the same place. This meant I wouldn't have to carry my pack even on the last day after he'd gone, so that was brilliant. My feet are bad again, the right little toe is now painful and the blister on my left heel has enlarged itself. So these two days of short mileage and no pack are just in the nick of time.

We booked into the *Swan Hotel* in the centre of Kington, friendly and quite cheap. Had delicious big steak and all the trimmings for supper.

Thursday 15 April
Kenchester - Bredwardine

We drove back to Kenchester and then I walked on to Bredwardine whilst Berwyn drove there and then came out to meet me. We hoped we'd meet at around the middle of Monnington Walk, and so we did! It was a beautiful day and a beautiful walk through apple orchards and well-tended farmland. We'd been to Bredwardine before, some years ago when we'd spent a long weekend visiting places connected with Kilvert of Kilvert's Diary fame: Clyro, Hay-on-Wye and Bredwardine. I'd read his diary, which inspired a real wish to see the places he wrote about. On that visit we stayed at the Rhyddspence Inn and I remember the landlord asking us whether we'd come for the walking or for Kilvert. 'For Kilvert,' I'd replied with some surprise, because it had never occurred to me that you might go somewhere just for the pleasure of its walking! Which just goes to show how we evolve in our lives. We passed by the Rhyddspence Inn this time and it brought back a flood of memories. Our milk jug at home came from Kilvert's house in Clyro, which was flourishing as an Art and Crafts centre, and perhaps still is. I'm still very fond of Kilvert and it was great to walk along the lanes and paths he would have travelled. Bredwardine became his parish for a while before he died and he is buried there. And it was because of Kilvert that we'd arranged to meet this morning in Monnington Walk.

Later, we drove on to Hay-on-Wye and did a bit of browsing in bookshops (me) and antique shops (Berwyn) while the washing was doing in the launderette. There was a quite smart little dress shop and Berwyn bought me a silk shirt to wear when I finally finish the walk and can wear proper clothes again!

Funnily enough, I kept thinking that by tomorrow Berwyn will have gone home again. I was reminded of the boarding school philosophy adhered to by headmasters of boys' prep schools - no visiting for the first several weeks because it 'upsets the boys.' I always used to think that was awful. Surely it would be better to let the boys see their parents even if it did upset them. But it was exactly that feeling I was having. I'd been so looking forward to seeing Berwyn, and then, by the second day, all I could think of was that by this time tomorrow he'll have gone again. Anyway, Bredwardine will be even more special now, full of memories.

Friday 16 April
Bredwardine - Kington

Berwyn dropped me off at Bredwardine and continued on to Sussex. He got home about 3pm apparently, and that was exactly the time I walked into Kington, this time getting there on foot for the first time. And what a difference it makes! I got a completely different idea of the place, arriving from across the fields and lanes all the way from Bredwardine. It looked altogether a more attractive and welcoming place.

From Bredwardine I walked to Whitney-on-Wye, first through quiet Kilvert lanes and then across the fields via a footpath to the toll-bridge across the Wye. After crossing the bridge and the A368 I followed a footpath going straight up the steep hill going through the woods to Brilley. This was quite high up and I had splendid views of the Black Mountains and Wales. From there I followed the little lanes into Kington, total about 13 miles. Huge thick black clouds followed me all the way, but I got to Kington before even a spot fell.

I was very pleased with today's walk, which is my own route. The Wye Valley Walk was excellent and on the whole easy to follow, but it's good to be travelling again on my specially tailored long-distance path!

It's like another world in all these places, so quiet and gentle and civilized. I feel swept back in time at least 30 years. People are very friendly; they smile at you as they drive past in their cars and always pass the time of day when you meet them.

Saturday 17 April
Kington - Knighton

This morning my very nice landlady of the last three nights gave me £5 for the LRF, and a little homily on how I must find a way to tell people about what I'm doing and why. I had told her daughter about the walk in the course of a conversation last night, but my landlady was concerned that I might have left without her knowing. She wanted to make a contribution and said other people would feel that way too. She made me promise I'd tell people, made it sound as though it was my duty to do so. So I said I would. I do tell people about Jim of course, if they ask specific questions about why I'm doing the walk, but more often than not the communications I have with landladies and people I meet on the way are quite brief and business-like.

Now I'm into Wales once more (Powys) and this was an eventful day! I had company! It was my Offa's Dyke Path day and I was doing well for the first couple of miles out of Kington. Then I came to a great wide Sound of Musicy hillside and though I could see what I supposed was the Dyke running along the top, I didn't know whether to follow it to the right or left. Luckily, a little group of walkers appeared just at that moment and so I asked them the way. They'd also come from Kington, but along a different route, and as they were going to Knighton too, they invited me to join them. I felt they might be just being polite and wouldn't really want a stray female tagging along holding them up, but on the other hand it was a bit awkward to follow along a few yards to the rear. So I trotted along at the back for a bit but eventually ended up walking all the way to Knighton with them and it was great fun. I also had a totally irresponsible day in terms of map-reading. My five gentlemen friends[20] were all seasoned walkers and ultra-efficient map-readers; one of them had already walked the whole length of the Offa's Dyke Path some years ago. So we ambled along very happily together and they were so nice and friendly.

It was misty at first but became clearer and there were panoramic views down into wide, sweeping, sheep-dotted valleys, and beyond to the dark, distant Welsh mountains. My companions told me this was one of the best sections of the Offa's Dyke and it certainly was

---

20. One of them later sent me a donation to the LRF, collected from his home town Rotary Club.

beautiful. It was quite steep in places, but well marked. I think I would have managed to follow all the acorns had I been on my own, but my gentlemen friends had all the booklets, maps and far more information than I'd got, so I had no cares. Four of them were retired bank managers and one was a computer expert. The latter, who was Chinese, was the Jim'll Fix It of their party, prepared for every eventuality, his rucksack bursting with the wherewithal for running repairs to person, camera, spectacles - anything that might conceivably need his attention. I heard that it was because of his presence on their walk that the left-behind wives were not overly concerned about the welfare of their menfolk.

At about midday we stopped for something to eat and took photos of each other before setting off again. By the time we were nearly there, we felt we all knew each other quite well and we were a very merry party as we came down off the Offa's Dyke into Knighton. Full of hilarity and mock gallantry, they insisted on seeing me to the very door of my B&B, where they gave my landlady a fit by suggesting that they had come to stay too! She took them at their word of course and told them she was full up, whereupon they burst out laughing and said that was alright - they'd share with me! It was good fun and made quite a change for me. They were impressed with what I was doing and said I'd set them a cracking pace! (I didn't - I was slower than they were really). They were on the last day of their walk and were going to take a taxi back to Chepstow, and then home to Paddock Wood, Maidstone and Essex.

It's very clean and smart here and my boots have been locked into the garden shed. My landlady wanted me to take off my rucksack on our way to the bedroom, and when I said I preferred to keep it on because it's so heavy, she asked me to please mind the pictures. Unfortunately several little pieces of mud dropped to the floor in the sparkling clean bedroom as I took my pack off, and I felt awful as she picked up a little chunk between her fingertips, exclaiming 'Oh dear! What's this?' I launched into a garbled explanation of how we'd had to push an old man's car out of a ditch, an event that had resulted in me catching most of the mud flung up when the wheels began to spin. It was true, but I could tell she was thinking, 'We've got a right one here', especially after the hilarity of my arrival!

I had a very slow supper in the Lantern Tea Rooms. We were only three people in there and I can't think what would happen if they ever got a rush on. At least 10 minutes went by before they even took my order, and then another 20 minutes before the food came. The other couple eating there were also from my B&B, having travelled all the way from Yorkshire to buy a telescope.

Sunday 18 April
Knighton - Clun

Next morning my landlady was really sweet and friendly. She had a great interest in geology and precious stones and gave me a geode on a key ring, a travel keep-safe stone. Another landlady who wants a postcard from John O'Groats.

Back up onto the Offa's Dyke Path, just as far as Treverward. A lot of this section is actually on the Dyke and it's amazing to think how old it is, 740 AD or thereabouts I think. I went into the Offa's Dyke Centre at Knighton and found out that each person was required to dig a stretch four feet long, then he could go home.

At Treverward I turned off to travel down the lanes to Clun, by which time I was back in England again, Shropshire now. It was a lovely walk, only eight miles, and the views were magnificent. Took lots of pictures but I dare say they won't do it justice. The morning's walk on Offa's Dyke was occasionally very steep, like yesterday, and I think that may have been the cause of a brand new ailment, an area of raw red skin on my back. Walking up the steep bits with a bent back probably caused my pack to rub against my spine. It's quite painful.

I got to Clun about 2.30pm and met Joanna and John[21] as arranged. They had already arrived at the Buffalo Inn where we're all staying. It's a lovely old inn, right in the centre of Clun, owned and run by friends of Joanna's. Brenda and Lorne are really sweet and suggested that we stay two nights and they'll drive me back to Church Stretton on Tuesday morning. They also insist I don't pay, but put the money instead into the LRF.

Later on, I walked four miles of tomorrow's journey so it won't be so long; it would have been a 16-mile stretch to Church Stretton and some of it quite steep.

---

21. Joanna, a friend for many years, since we collected children at the primary school gates. John, her partner.

We had a big dinner cooked by Brenda and Lorne and they joined us when they could. They introduced us to some of the local inhabitants and it was altogether quite festive. Joanna was on good form, though slightly apprehensive about tomorrow's walk.

This morning as I was approaching Clun, I had my first glimpse of the Long Mynd (it's pronounced rhyming with 'wind', not 'kind' as I had been doing). It's instantly recognizable and I was thrilled to see it. I'd read about it in the footpath book[22], and it also figures in a book describing all the wild places in Britain[23]. It sounded remote and glorious and I was determined to include the Shropshire Hills, and that particular hill, in my route. It may even have been the first of the 'must-see' places. The countryside all around is spectacularly beautiful and I'm so pleased I chose to come this way.

It's a lucky place too, because it was as I was walking down from the Offa's Dyke, gazing at the view of the Long Mynd, that the idea of the book sprang into my mind. I would write up a description of this walk when I get home, just a slim volume, containing all the map numbers, mileage, long-distance paths taken and so on. A factual account of this, my route, which I'm very pleased with so far. It's both scenic and varied, and a good mixture of long-distance paths and lanes. I am sure that varying the route is an important factor. To follow a long-distance path in its entirety, the South-West Coastal Path for example, or the Pennine Way, mile upon mile for days on end, would for me, be tedious. Also I feel I'd cease to appreciate the great panoramas of its scenery, however splendid, simply because I'd become habituated to it. So I am resolved to write up my good and varied route, which will be for people like me, novice walkers who have a liking for wild and beautiful countryside, but who are not very intrepid. And there is a need for such a book; the idea came because so many people have asked me if there is a recognized route to follow. In fact, as I found out, there is surprisingly little information on walking from Land's End to John O'Groats. Planning the route and acquiring the appropriate maps took up most of last winter and I loved doing it, but many people haven't the time, so a prepared and tested journey could be just what's needed. And since I have all the information at my computer-tips, as it were, it would be easy to do.

22. *The Footpaths of Britain*, by Michael Marriott. Blitz Editions, 1981.
23. *Wild Britain*, by Douglas Botting. Ebury Press, 1988.

Monday 19 April
Clun - Church Stretton

Clun to Church Stretton was the original day's walk, but because of my yesterday's extra miles Joanna and I only had to go from the Bury Ditches car park (four miles out of Clun). In fact we did the walk in reverse because Lorne could drive us to Church Stretton in the morning more easily than he could collect us from there in the evening. So we set off from Church Stretton at a good pace up the steep ascent to the Long Mynd. There was a cold wind with patchy sun and it was dry. We climbed up quite quickly as there was a tarmac road for several miles, leading to a Gliding Club. The gliders were being winched up every few minutes and we had to make a detour so as not to be hit by the winch returning to the ground. We also kept our eyes peeled for the gliders themselves, as last year a woman was killed by one that went into her from behind. It's a horrific thought - I suppose you just wouldn't hear it coming. And pretty awful for the pilot too, seeing a person there and apparently not able to steer away from her.

We were hugely impressed with the panoramic views from the top of the Long Mynd. You could see for miles, southeast towards the Cotswolds in one direction and westwards to the Brecon Beacons and Snowdonia in the other.

Joanna was pleased with her day! She was terrific really, because apparently she'd been quite anxious that she wouldn't be able to do it, and so had done some serious training throughout the previous weeks. She also did a great job getting sponsorships. She was the first person to book herself in to join me for a day on the walk, and I remember being quite surprised and touched by her determination. She walks with fast little steps and was absolutely fine on the walk, though tired by the end.

Tuesday 20 April
Church Stretton - Shrewsbury

Change of plan. I ditched the day off planned for Church Stretton because I'd rather shorten some of the days ahead. Terrible weather, it was non-stop torrential rain from start to finish. The thought of Brenda's packed lunch lurked at the back of my mind all day, and I was continuously on the lookout for somewhere to eat it. Even tried getting in to a church, but it was locked. At about 4pm I stood under a tree and managed to eat the crisps and a tomato. But basically it was head down, smothered in waterproof (even put my gaiters on for the first time) and walk without stopping. I arrived here, the first B&B I saw, completely knackered and sopping wet. But I've now got my waterproof anorak that Berwyn brought up on his last visit, and so together with my absolutely excellent Paramo trousers, am as dry as a bone inside. Boots wet inside for the first time. My room is tiny and I'm a bit pushed to find enough places to spread my dripping clothes and mackintosh covers. I suppose I ought to have asked the landlord if I could hang them downstairs somewhere, but I was too exhausted to do anything except get my clobber off and sink onto the bed. Finally got to eat my packed lunch in bed, blessing Brenda, because I'd never have had the energy to go out again to find food.

I went through some lovely countryside but because of the teeming rain it wasn't possible to appreciate it to the full. Hawthorne in full leaf now.

The River Severn has flooded six times in the last 12 months at Shrewsbury. A scheme to dredge it to enable small craft to use it is too expensive (Local news).

Wednesday 21 April
Shrewsbury - Wem

Another quite big day (at least 14 miles) but the weather improved and I felt much better. Had an enormous 11-hour sleep last night, from soon after 9pm till 8.20am! Only just woke up in time for breakfast. Another very nice couple were staying at the B&B, husband interested in the technicalities of the walk, how many miles per day, miles per hour etc. and wife wanting to know why I'm doing it. When I told her, her eyes filled with tears. People are amazing in their compassion and generosity. I think I always knew this, but it's being spelt out to me now (or should I say dealt out to me)!

I've realised that I get back into my normal walking groove very quickly when I'm on my own. It's great to have company and I love seeing family and friends, but when they've gone I revert almost immediately to what now seems normal life. The days are low-key and matter of fact, walking at a steady pace, sometimes observing the scenery all around, sometimes lost in my own thoughts. I'm always aware of wild life though, birds particularly. Most of all, on my own I think about Jim. Not necessarily the sad things and the weeks of his illness, but quite often about happy times and his character. I also ponder a lot on why he got ill, and run through all the possible contributory factors. Useless thoughts really. Sometimes I just let myself visualize him, or hear his voice on the telephone, 'Hello Mum, Jim here.' I say it out loud and try to imitate the exact tone of his voice. Then I think, *where* is he - what's he *doing*? Like I was always saying in Stonegate churchyard, what are you *doing* here Jim-a-long?

Anyway, the thing is, that it's good and right that I'm walking on my own, because these times are the essence of what it's all about. Plus I love seeing all the different shades of countryside, much more noticeable when you're on your own. Today was flattish arable land and I've been reminded sometimes of Thoroton, sometimes Ripe[24].

I absolutely love this farmy countryside, old-fashioned, lush and incredibly green. Tractors parked outside the farm cottages at lunchtime. Little red-brick houses and beautiful black and white timbered houses predominate. The lower halves of churches and the more substantial houses are made up of huge blocks of red stone. The horse chestnuts are in leaf and in one sheltered nook the May blossom was just coming out. Smelt that slightly wiffy but very nostalgic scent for the first time.

Didn't bother trying to find the Shropshire Way because the lanes were lovely to walk through and because it was so wet everywhere. The lanes were quite often flooded, so it would have been a real trudge across the fields. Also I needed to get going quite fast as I had a lot of Shrewsbury to get through before I even started the 12 miles to Wem. Did a bit of shopping in Shrewsbury (Shroosbury, as they say here). Bought Tam a pretty embroidered nightie for her birthday in one of the very tempting boutiques in the town centre.

No supper tonight and only crisps for lunch so I'm looking forward to the big breakfast tomorrow! Had quite a job finding a B&B. Don't like Wem. It has a horrible main street, and the places I went into to enquire about B&B were unhelpful, and they looked at me as if I was a freak. Eventually found a place a mile out of town (back the way I'd come) so couldn't be bothered to go out again. Shorter day tomorrow.

24. Ripe in East Sussex; Thoroton in the Vale of Belvoir, Nottinghamshire. Two of the places where I lived as a child.

Thursday 22 April
Wem - Whitchurch

With the weather a bit better and a shorter journey, I decided to crack the Shropshire Way. All went well, and I joined it after turning off the Whitchurch road at Creamore Farm. The path went through meadows and farmyards, interspersed with lanes. The lanes were all mud and manure, the houses surrounded by collapsing agricultural buildings, some of them beautiful. It's the sort of country I love. I lost the path for a bit, but it didn't matter; not only are the intervening lanes easy to walk along and virtually traffic-free, it also gave my boots a chance to dry off a bit. The fields were very boggy and wet.

The only nerve-racking moment of the day came when I suddenly found myself face to face with an enormous bull! The field was full of cows and I was padding along, concentrating on the map to see which direction to take for the next way-mark (white buzzard) or stile, when I glanced up - and there, only a few feet away, was this huge bull, ring through his nose, looking at me! He shifted his back legs and started to do an enormous pee and I thought 'my God! He's preparing for action!' I stood stock-still and we looked at each other a bit longer. My over-riding urge was to run like hell, but I thought it would be better to put the distance between us in a more casual manner, and so made my way as nonchalantly as possible towards the nearest fence, which I now noticed was electric. It also crossed my mind he might be wondering if I was a new type of cow, because I had the grey mackintosh cover on my rucksack which makes it look huge as it rustles and flaps in the wind! But nothing happened and after several minutes of faster and faster walking and muttering things like 'Oh help' and worse, under my breath, I realised he wasn't at all interested in me. The cows and some of the young heifers were, but I can cope with them. All the same I was very relieved to reach the gate - any gate, way-marked with a buzzard or not!

I left the Shropshire Way at Alkington where there was a beautiful farm and Hall, the latter Tudor I think. Little roads took me soon into Whitchurch, and with not a B&B in sight I welcomed the Tourist Information sign. They found me a good B&B, about a mile out of town, £15, good for this area. Another luxurious bathroom (peach) and lavish decoration. The landlady had extracted all the information out of me within the first two minutes; I hadn't even got as far as the bedroom or got my pack off! But she was very nice and said all the usual things like 'Oooh! All on yerown?' It's this, the fact that I'm walking on my own, that really knocks them out.

A note about B&B landladies: they're such a kind, wholesome lot. Often married to builders or farmers, or they're retired. They can't do enough for you and several of them have been moved to tears when they hear about Jim. Their houses are nearly always stuffed full of furniture and knick-knacks and home comforts. Clean and spruce, and decorated to the hilt.

Last day in Shropshire.

Friday 23 April
Whitchurch - Tarporley

I set off with the intention of following the Sandstone Trail towards Tarporley, and stopping for the night somewhere on the way, as it's a 16-mile walk and this was the reason I'd cancelled my day-off in Church Stretton. So, I joined the Sandstone Trail at Willey Moor lock, a short cut from my B&B recommended by my landlady's husband. This cut off a mile but meant that I missed the three miles of the Llangollen Branch of the Shropshire Union Canal which I'd been looking forward to, because the Sandstone Trail leaves the Canal at that point and goes across farmland. Never mind, there'll be plenty more canals to come. It was very wet and misty but it's the best-marked long-distance path I've come across, certainly much better than the Shropshire Way. The way-mark of a black boot on a yellow disk was easily spotted and frequent enough for me not to be wandering around squinting at the hedgerows wondering where the next stile or gate might be.

I ditched the higher parts of the walk (which is a section of a McCloy route) partly because the weather was so closed in I wouldn't have been able to see the mountains of North Wales anyway, and partly because of time. There were no B&Bs and it gradually became apparent that I was going to have to walk all the way to Tarporley after all. In the end the day's walk was five miles of Sandstone Trail, eight miles of lanes, and another three miles of Sandstone Trail and local footpaths to Tarporley.

I was seizing up by the time I got to Tarporley and then couldn't find a B&B here either. The one place I knew about was fully booked and so I was very relieved to get into the Crown Inn. I've just had a huge meal of butterflied chicken breast marinated in juicy Caribbean spices. It was called Chicken Jerk!

Tomorrow I get nearer still to urban areas. 'Frodgeham', as it's pronounced, is on the Mersey estuary. Dan couldn't believe I was so far north when I phoned him just now! I can hardly believe it myself. I crossed the Shropshire Union Canal just outside Tarporley and the day after tomorrow there will be lots more canal walks. I think I am to low-level water walks what McCloy is to high-level hills! He loves the mountains and doesn't want you to miss a hill! And to think I've missed all those Bulkeley and Peckforth hills today - all I've done is look at them from the valley! He (McCloy) more or less apologises for the fact that the first three miles of the Sandstone Trail follow the Llangollen Canal, whereas to me that was a positive enticement and would make up for the wooded heights to follow.

I've been thinking - it's the knowledge that I've got such a lot at home that really enabled me to do this trip. Had I not had such a broad base of love and family-togetherness I would never have risked it. The people who are really brave are the ones who set off totally isolated. It's easy to do anything if there's a haven of love and acceptance in the background. I suppose that's roughly what I wanted the boys to have. I read once that the best way to bring up children was simply to love them and leave them. Not an easy thing to do, it was suggested. It was easy to love them of course, and I think I interpreted the leaving them bit as letting them do what they want, in their own way, sixties person that I was, though I wasn't aware of the sixties culture at the time.

My legs are in a state of rash again, as after the big day to Portishead. It seems that if I do more than 15 miles my legs protest visibly! Also they ache, and as in Portishead, I'm aware of the blood rushing around in them.

Crossed into Cheshire soon after Whitchurch.

Still *Midlands Today* (TV local news).

Map

- Carlisle
- Caldbeck
- Orthwaite
- Keswick
- Stonethwaite
- Dungeon Ghyll
- Coniston
- Newby Bridge
- Grange over Sands
- Warton
- Caton
- Abbeystead
- Slaidburn
- Hurst Green
- Blackburn
- Horwich
- Glazebury
- Stockton Heath
- Frodsham
- Tarporley

LIVERPOOL

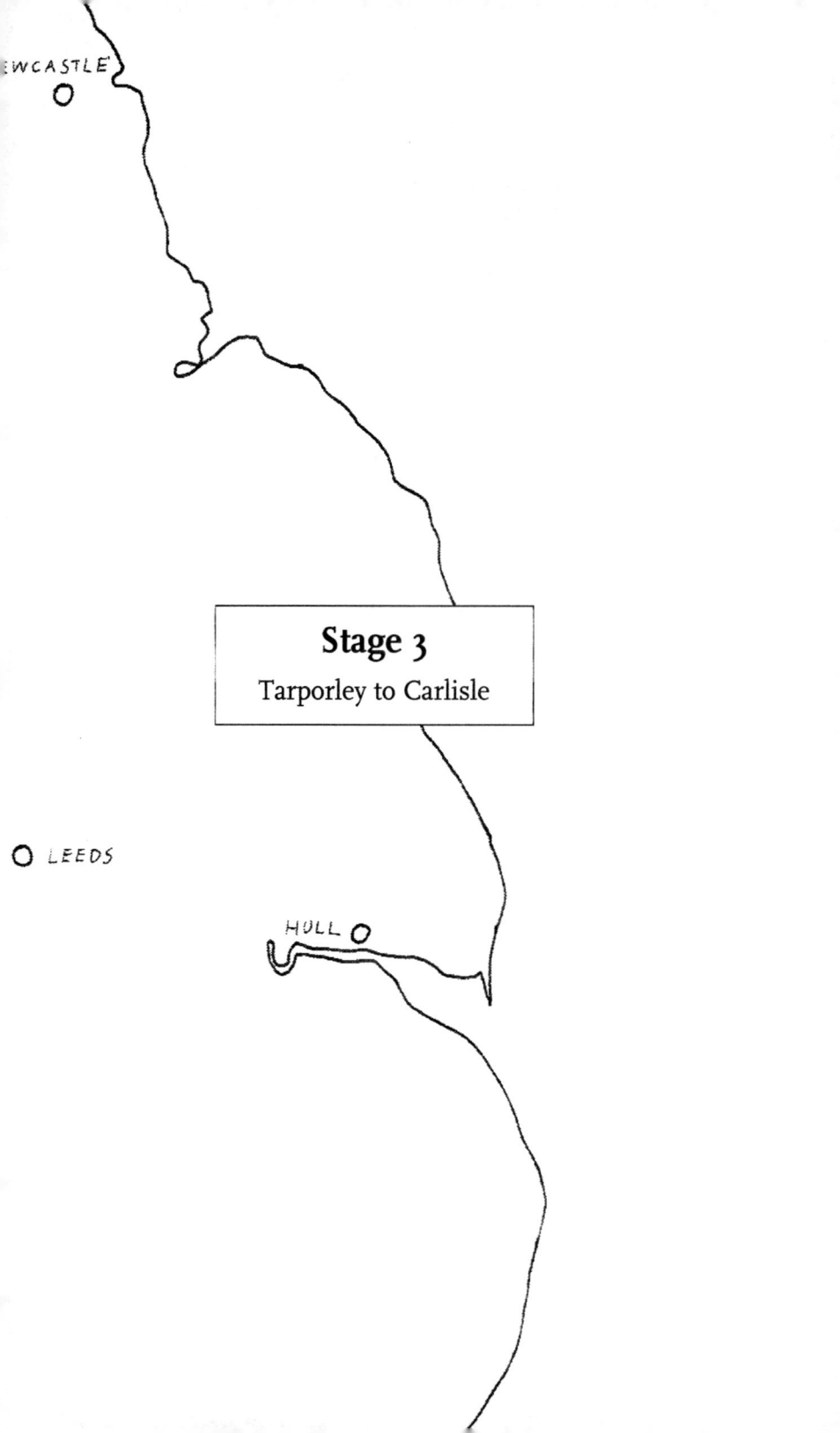

Stage 3
Tarporley to Carlisle

Tarporley to Carlisle

Canals - Forest of Bowland - Lake District
Saturday, 24 April - Saturday, 15 May

OS 117 Chester

Tarporley, *Sandstone Trail* to Primrosehill Wood,
Delamere Forest, **Frodsham**. 13 miles

OS117 + 108 Liverpool + 109 Manchester

Frodsham, River Weaver, Dutton, *Cheshire Ring Canal Walk*,
Preston Tunnel, Moore, Hr. & Lr. Walton, **Stockton Heath**. 14 miles

Stockton Heath, *Cheshire Ring Canal Walk*, Lymm,
Warburton, Man.Ship Canal toll bridge, Rixton Claypits,
Glazebrook, **Glazebury**. 14 miles

Glazebury, Leigh, Leeds & Liverpool Canal, Dover,
Platt Bridge, Aspull, **Horwich**. 14 miles

OS 109 + 103 Blackburn

Horwich, Rivington Reservoir, White Coppice, Brinscall,
Withnell, **Blackburn**. 15 miles

Blackburn, Pleasington, Woodcock Hill, Mellor, Park Gate,
Ribchester Bridge, Marles Wood, River Ribble path,
Dinckley footbridge, **Hurst Green**. 12 miles

Hurst Green, Lower Hodder Bridge, Bashall Eaves,
Cow Ark, Longstripes, Whiteholme, **Slaidburn**. 13 miles

OS 103 + 102 Preston, Blackpool

Slaidburn, Dunsop Bridge, Trough of Bowland,
Tower Lodge, **Abbeystead**. 12 miles

OS 102 + 97 Kendal

Abbeystead, Quernmore, **Caton**.	8 miles
Caton, **Warton**.	7 miles
Warton, Silverdale, Arnside, **Grange over Sands**.	8 miles
Grange over Sands, Cartmel, **Newby Bridge**.	7 miles
Newby Bridge, Sunny Bank, *Cumbria Way*, **Coniston**.	15 miles
Coniston, Tarn Hows, Elterwater, **Dungeon Ghyll**.	11 miles
Dungeon Ghyll, Stake Pass, **Stonethwaite**.	7 miles
Stonethwaite, **Keswick**.	8 miles
Keswick, Skiddaw, **Orthwaite**.	10 miles
Orthwaite, **Caldbeck**.	7 miles
Caldbeck, **Carlisle**, end of *Cumbria Way*.	15 miles
Total	**210 miles**

(19 days walking, average 11 miles per day. Days off: 3).

The Trent and Mersey canal
at Preston Brook.

Stage III

Saturday 24 April
Tarporley - Frodsham

A small disaster struck today. I was going well, on the Sandstone Trail negotiating Delamere Forest (where even McCloy admitted to getting lost) when bang! I fell flat on the ground, landing with terrific force on my HEAD of all things. I'd been trying to unhook my specs from the rucksack strap where I rather precariously balance them whilst taking a photo. My specs have got bent so many times and I'd be lost without them, so I was concentrating on them and not looking where I was going. The path was full of protruding tree roots and I was stupid not to stop. So there I was, spread-eagled on the forest floor, head hurting like mad and blood all over the place! My first thought was to stop the bleeding - well, it may not have been my initial reaction, but it was my first constructive thought. I fumbled around in my pocket for tissues and pressed, not too hard, on my head - and then felt even worse because of the appalling amount of blood that ensued. It was so bright, and I was thinking is this arterial blood, and will it all end here? But the worst bleeding eventually stopped and I knew that at least I hadn't cut an artery. I sat up gingerly (my ankle was hurting too) and feeling rather sick, like Peter Rabbit, drank some water. Then, after another 10 minutes or so I thought, well - there's only one thing to be done: carry on walking! I did feel a bit shaky, and walked slowly and very carefully so as not to exert any pressure on my head that would re-start the bleeding. I passed a few people over the next mile or so of forest and considered asking them for help, but what would be the point? If they whisked me away in their car to get stitched up in the nearest A&E department, I'd only have to return to this spot the next day and do that bit of the walk. And we'd have to get to their car first and I'd long since gone past all the car parks. So I thought I'd get to the nearest road and find a B&B.

No B&Bs. I've only seen one B&B in the whole of Cheshire, and that was all shut up. Eventually I walked the remaining three or four miles to Frodsham and had my first glimpse of the Mersey from a hill above the town. I enquired of a police-car parked by the side of the road where the nearest A&E was and was told five or seven miles away, depending. They were not interested in bleeding heads and so I continued down the hill into the town of Frodsham, which was not very nice, dirty and full of stares. Still no B&Bs. After rejecting all the seedy-looking pubs in the town centre I enquired the price at a fairly ordinary but clean-looking small hotel. £45 for a single B&B was the staggering reply. The receptionist was helpful however and when I asked if she knew of anywhere cheaper, rang up the Robin Hood, four miles away in Helsby. She booked it for me and was very kind, gave me a glass of water when I explained what had happened. We had a cosy chat about the lack of B&Bs and the expense of any reasonable accommodation, which she blamed squarely on the business population who don't have to pay for themselves. The upshot was, I got the bus to Helsby (because it's off my route and I'll return by it to Frodsham the day after tomorrow) and I'm settled in here for today and tomorrow, so I can rest up. I've washed most of the blood off my clothes and neck and arms but can't bring myself to do much about my head. I've phoned Berwyn a few times and I badly want to see him, but there would be no point in him coming all this way.

North West Tonight TV local news.

Sunday 25 April
Day off; Helsby

Thank goodness I had my saved-up day off in which to recuperate. It would have been hard indeed to walk 12 miles today. Don't feel very good. I still don't know what the cut looks like because it's on the top and towards the back of my head so I can't see it. I've been wondering if it was caused by Stick? I might have trodden on the base of it as I was falling, thereby causing it to smash down onto my head. I can't think how else I'd have such a big cut in that place. I washed off some of the blood last night and I'll have another go tonight. I don't want to risk starting off the bleeding again though. Handfuls of hair have come out from a graze on the front of my head too. I found out from the hotel that there are no A&E departments nearer than Runcorn which is several miles away, and I'm certainly not wasting money on a taxi (no buses on a Sunday). It's getting better anyway, though my head and neck ache terribly and

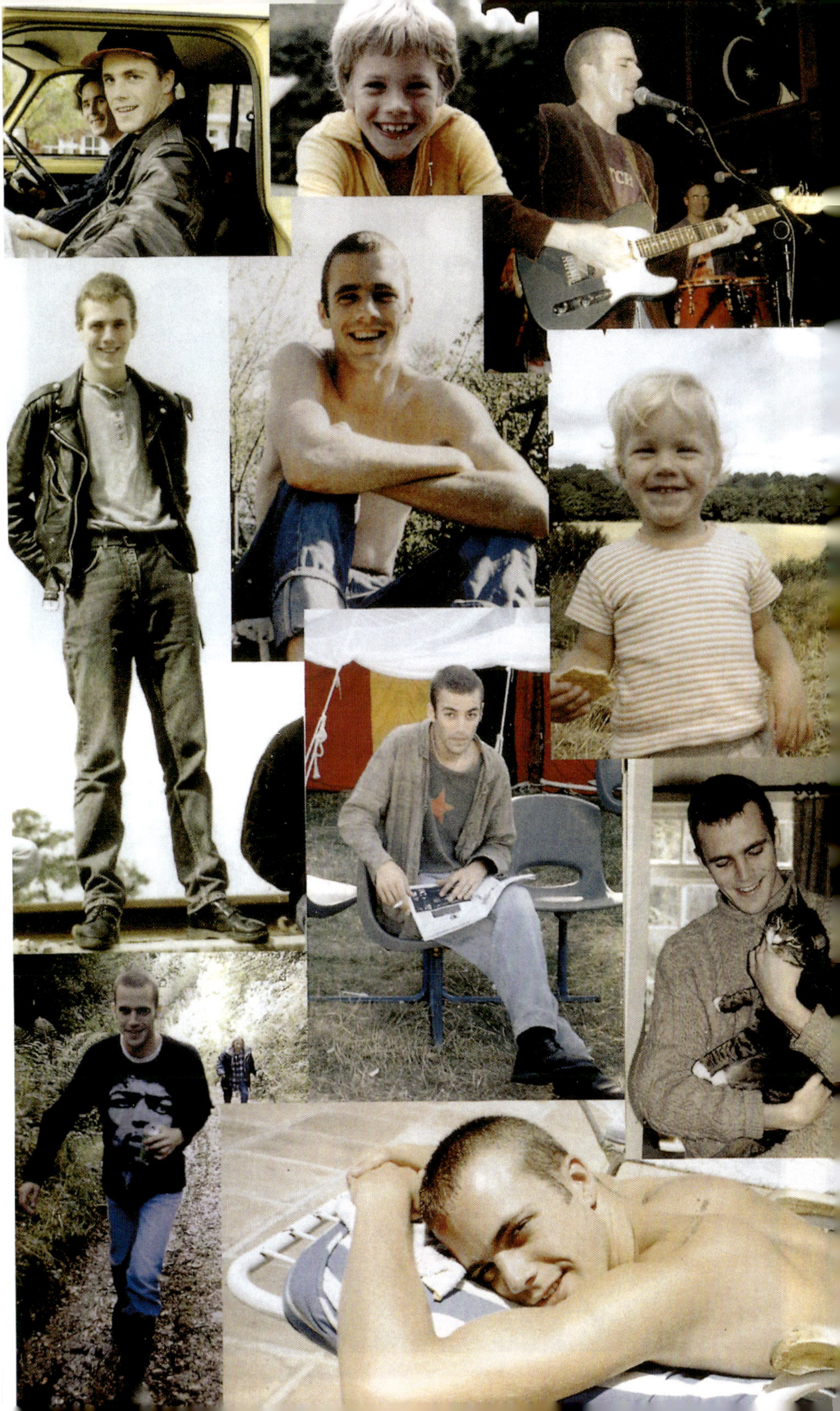

Sally, David, Michael, Tam arriving at John O'Groats.

Tam, Michael, Sally, David arrive home to a big Welcome.

my neck is as stiff as a plank. I'm sure the best thing is to rest. Animals don't wash their wounds in water or mess about with dressings after all, they just rest and nature heals them.

After today, though, I'll have to keep to my schedule in order to reach Slaidburn in a week's time where I've got two nights booked into the youth hostel. Can't believe that in a week I'll be right in my Forest of Bowland, and that will mean I'm at the halfway mark! Dunsop Bridge is, according to the Ordnance Survey people, the exact centre of the British Isles. Good that my reckonings tally with theirs!

A note about the Sandstone Trail: it's very good. Absolutely no bother about picking it up after leaving it to stay in Tarporley, and clearly marked as previously. Often the walk really is on sandstone, a gritty reddish sort of sand, easy on the feet. Yesterday's route was mostly wooded, Primrose Hill Wood, Nettleford Wood and finally the fated Delamere Forest. And though I'm not usually keen on woody walks these were OK, the conifers interspersed with old deciduous trees and some open stretches. I saw a great spotted woodpecker - it landed in a tree right next to me, and then realizing its mistake, flew off in a gorgeous flash of red feathers. The birdsong was lovely throughout, except in Primrose Hill Wood, which was being cut and was all conifers anyway. In fact, Primrose Hill Wood wasn't as good as the name implied, there was a lengthy diversion because of all the chopping and it was slippery and wet - I fell down there too, I've just remembered.

So after a day of rest and feeling sorry for myself, I hope by tomorrow I'll have reaped the benefits. It should be an easy walk, flat, and best of all, it will be going along the canal towpaths that I've been looking forward to so much. Corrers tonight!

Monday 26 April
Frodsham - Stockton Heath

Felt quite a lot better this morning, neck ache not so bad and headache gone. I got the bus back to Frodsham and was glad to get out of that slightly depressing inn, though it was comfortable enough.

Downpours of rain all morning. From Frodsham there were a couple of miles of main road walking before turning off onto the footpath by the River Weaver. And from there until I arrived here at about 4 pm, it was river or canal towpaths all the way. First along the banks of the River Weaver and the Weaver navigation, meadows of Friesian cows grazing the lush wet grass to the left of me, woods carpeted with bluebells and wild garlic to the right. At Dutton Lock, half a mile of bridleway linked up to the Trent and Mersey Canal, which then took me all the way to Preston Brook. Here, a man in a canal barge offered me my first lift of the whole trip. I explained I couldn't accept, but it was a kind offer and in other circumstances I would certainly have accepted (there being no towpath through the tunnel). In McCloy's day you had to do a couple of miles road-walking at this juncture, but now the lane going to the north side of the Preston Tunnel is just across the road (next to the Talbot Arms pub).

At Preston Marina the canal became the Bridgewater Canal, the oldest canal of all, and I stayed on that all the way to Stockton Heath. Tried in vain to find B&Bs in all the places I passed through - Moore, Lower Walton and Higher Walton. Asking in the Post Office or newsagents always gets the same reply: 'nothing like that round here love.' Here in Stockton there are a few hotels and this one is the least posh, but even so it's £30 for a miniscule box of a bedroom. This is a 'special price' for me; normal business rate would be £38! I have a bathroom along the corridor, the entire space of which (loo, shower and a 4 x 9inch basin) would fit into a normal shower unit. You have to be a contortionist to do anything and my elbows are black and blue from crashing them against the door, the shower handle, the taps.... Earlier on, as I went out to look for food, I saw a carload of Japanese businessmen letting themselves in to the front door of the main house (I'm in the annexe), and blamed them for the exorbitant price! But it's only a couple of miles from Warrington and not much further to Manchester and so I suppose it's to be expected. The traffic is incredible and it took forever to cross the road.

Today's journey was a miracle of quiet considering how close I was to all this. I noticed how the sound of traffic carries though, the M56 passed over the canal at one point and the sound of it was continuous and lingered on for miles. By contrast, Virgin Intercity trains flashed past on the mainline railway every 20 minutes or so and left complete silence in their wake.

I can feel great lumps of caked blood on my head still, but it's not so sore now.

Tuesday 27 April
Stockton Heath - Glazebury

Depressed beyond words - literally! Didn't have the energy even to write the one word, *horrible*, last night, which is all I would have written. Except for the accident day, it was the worst so far. I'm writing all this the next day.

The morning was quite good: six or seven miles along the gentle Bridgewater Canal, and that, like the previous day's walk, was lovely. The weather was sunny and not too hot, but I was walking into a strong easterly wind, which made it a bit tiring. Then north through the suburbs again, roads all the way except for one relatively pastoral (unofficial) footpath that led to Warburton and the toll bridge over the Manchester Ship Canal. I was especially pleased to see that, a name out of the past and so familiar from geography O levels. These canals are magnificent, so clean-looking and a joy to walk along. Took a picture of the Trafford Borough of Manchester sign for Dan[25]. Warburton was a sleepy little village and I sat awhile under the shade of the churchyard trees. Heard the cuckoo again as I meandered through the patchy sort of countryside, areas of scrubland interspersed with garages, meadows and a few fields of rape. Didn't meet a soul.

Then things started to go badly. After crossing the Manchester Ship canal, it was a long, hard road slog, getting progressively built up, so I was glad to find the footpath that should have been a short cut through a farm and then out across the fields the other side of the motorway. The farm was run-down and bedraggled, housing only a few horses. I crossed the bridge over the motorway and made my way into what I thought was a very boggy entrance to the next field. Then it dawned on me that I was making my way across an enormous slurry heap. This was the stuff of nightmares. It got worse and worse and I was completely stuck for a while. I persevered through quite a lot of it, even after I realised it was becoming a slurry tip, because it looked as though the ground ahead was more substantial. But as I got closer I realised it was even worse, the slurry not even padded out by the small lumps of rotted straw which was all that had saved me from sinking right into the stuff up till that point. My boots were

---

25. A Manchester United supporter.

already in it up to the ankle. After a bit I knew there was nothing for it - I had to turn round and go back the way I'd come, which was even harder because I'd sunk the few tufts of straw I'd used as stepping stones to get there. At one point, in desperation, I was wondering if I should remove my pack to lighten my weight, but couldn't bear the thought of it sinking without trace, and me ending up without a pack as well as half dead. There was no farm or habitation within sight, and nobody would have heard me shout for help because of the proximity of the motorway. In the end, heart in mouth and weak-kneed, I reached firmer ground again and retraced my steps back to the farm and the road. This was a footpath McCloy had used, but clearly it wasn't in that condition then. One footpath sign had fallen down and another was non-existent, so I should have been warned. So that little detour wasted an hour at least, made me very cross and tired, boots filthy and stinking. Then I had to re-cross the motorway and do the long road bit that I had been trying to avoid in the first place.

By the time I reached Glazebury, the morning's stroll along the gentle Bridgewater Canal seemed like weeks ago. And in terms of distance it was quite far: 14 miles without the detour and the mishap. I'd walked under the M6, over the M62 (twice) and the Manchester Ship Canal. Traffic everywhere was hotting up. I'd kept my eyes peeled for a B&B all the way from the manure disaster onwards, thinking I'd cheer myself by doing a shorter day. No such luck. Even in Glazebury there were no B&Bs so I had to try the pubs. After about four attempts, the Nags Head (not its real name) said, yes, they had accommodation, but would I wait till 5 pm whilst the landlady 'cleaned up the mess made by the gentleman who stayed here last night!' Eventually I was shown into the barest room I've ever seen - no side light, no tea, no TV, no chair, no nothing. There was a bathroom across the landing that was so dirty I had to clean the bath before I could bring myself to get into it, even with my aching, blood-rushing legs!

Downstairs in the bar there was a straggle of three or four men propping up the bar. Fixtures I think. Their conversation was unpleasant, everything tinged with murk and suspicion. It included a discussion of Jill Dando[26] and Princess Di, neither of whom were

---

26. Television presenter and personality, recently murdered on the steps of her London house.

'quite what they seemed' apparently. 'Nawbody is that clean and white, the way she's talked about' (Jill Dando). As for Di, 'that ginger-headed son of hers, he's not all he seems ... that captain in the Army', and so on. The topics turned to animals and specific remedies to cure the cat - 'stoof soom ginger oop 'is arse - that'd do the trick' and then what they'd do if they won the lottery. This last was actually rather pathetic. One of them would have bought a whole estate of houses, streets, shops and everything, so that he could make it a safe place for his grandson to run and play in. Another would move out of here, to Kent maybe, or Cornwall. Kent was the final choice.

I had another long wait in the bar for the supper that the landlady insisted on cooking for me. She was nice, poor thing, and the only one doing any work. The landlord spent his time talking to the fixtures and they were all a bit unfriendly and so I sat awkwardly in the lounge part. It was horrid. But by 8.30pm I was asleep!

Wednesday 28 April
Glazebury - Horwich (Bolton)

Looking at the map, the last couple of days have been a bit of a zig-zag to avoid the great urban areas of Runcorn, Warrington, Wigan, Bolton.

Today, another scenic canal-side walk in the morning was followed by another long road march in the second half of the day. Set off at 9am and had reached Leigh and the returning section of the Cheshire Ring Canal Walk, the Bridgewater Canal, soon after. Walking west along it now, and after a while it turned into the Leeds and Liverpool Canal. It got quite rural at Pennington Flash, where the huge lake and golf course gave way to wide-open spaces of heathery ground, dotted with ponds and small copses. Perfect for wildlife and in that stretch of four or five miles I saw so many birds I lost count - herons, gulls, ducks (all sorts), swans, geese, a hawk, moorhen, coots and lots I didn't know. The canal, dirtier now and lined by dark-brick Victorian warehouses and old mill-type buildings, still managed to look picturesque. Sadly my film had run out. The canal got progressively cleaner as it headed out through the country areas. One or two locks and only one longboat - a working barge piloted by a cheery bearded Scotsman who waved greetings at me.

I turned off the canal as it neared Wigan and went north again, padding quietly through the urban areas, for the most part avoiding the curious gaze of the local townsfolk. Got caught once though, whilst I was sitting on a bench swigging water - a friendly and fervent woman came up and blessed me, even before she knew what I was up to! She was agog when she knew and blessed me all over again.

The back-street route I'd chosen was a bit cheerless and seemed to go on for ever, so long before I reached Horwich I'd determined to put myself up in a HOTEL, as a cheer-up after yesterday, as a celebration because I've nearly reached the halfway mark, but most of all because I've felt so weary for the last few days. Normally I don't care too much where I sleep; so long as I find a bed I'm happy. But suddenly I found myself craving comfort and luxury. I would give myself a secular blessing! But the hotel marked on the map didn't exist, or at least I couldn't find it, even after going out of my way a couple of miles to look for it. So I was trudging along towards Horwich, thinking how expensive it would have been, and lining up all the other rationalizations for why another night in a seedy pub would be a Good Thing, when suddenly in front of me I saw the flags fluttering over a Holiday Inn! Glory halleluiah! I was in there like a flash - only to be completely devastated by the girl at Reception telling me 'Sorry, we're full up!' Mercifully, a second girl intervened at that point and said they did have one room left, and I swiftly clinched it by brandishing my credit card in front of their eyes. Perhaps they had a rule about not admitting dirty backpackers and then made an exception on seeing this poor old duck! I can't believe they were really full up; it's a massive place. The price is an incredible £47.50 a room, but it's a one-off and just what I need, as I keep telling myself!

I had a job to get into the room with this new-fangled cardboard key, but when I finally managed it the first thing I saw was a big notice on the computer screen saying 'Welcome Mrs Thomas!' I'm having a most luxurious time. The bathroom is bigger than the bedroom of most places, and the television as big as a shower. The shower is hot and powerful and I've used all the towels, washed my hair (carefully) and dried yesterdays washing with the hairdryer. My socks were already dry because I've taken to pinning them to the back of my rucksack, 'who cares if I look funny!' (Bugs Bunny). There's an enormous double bed and a sofa, all for me. I want to stay here forever!

Thursday 29 April
Horwich - Blackburn

7.30am: Last night I watched The Bridges of Madison County on the lovely whacking great TV. That was an excellent little book, but fairly insignificant as a film I thought. Clint Eastwood looks his age. Also, no horse and no cloak. Meryl Streep was good though.

Today I must try and cheer up. It's going to be a hot day. For the first time in my life I find myself wanting cool weather. Walking in the heat drains the energy and my pack seems the heaviest it's ever been (except at the beginning when I found it dreadfully heavy). At least I'll be moving out of the urban areas now and so hopefully there'll be some B&Bs.

Evening: It took ages to reach the shores of Rivington Reservoir. I must have mixed up the roads a bit because of all the new motorways and a vast new retail park and leisure centre under construction, not far from the Holiday Inn. The latter, by the way, was wonderfully clean and comfortable, but for that price I was astounded by the meagre breakfast - no cooked meal at all, just COLD croissant and rolls. Amazing, for all that money! I received some curious stares from all the black-suited business men staying there. There were a few black-suited business women too, but they didn't stare. Too busy.

Rivington and Anglezarke reservoirs were huge and blue when I finally reached them. The Tourist Information bureau at Rivington Reservoir was very useful and reassured me that I could go all the way along the eastern shore of the reservoirs, footpaths and bridleways all the way. Also she told me it was possible to get nearly as far as Brinscall up 'The Goit', a sort of drain going from the moors into the reservoir. So I changed the intended route a bit and did that, and was initially very pleased because the walk was beautiful, heathery landscape climbing gently, cows grazing, easy path and no people to speak of. But then, at White Coppice, there was a sign to Brinscall - turn *Right*. According to the map the way was straight on and all my instincts were to go straight on. It was a difficult decision because a lot of these 'permissive paths' are not marked on my map. The notice looked old and rusty - Ramblers Association 1963 - but there was a second, newer and very definite arrow fixed to it - Brinscall *Right.* So, after dithering for five minutes, I did. Wrong decision! One hour later, after climbing steadily all the time, puffing and blowing and in a lather of sweat, I was on top of the moors! Blooming heck! It was quite spectacular and the views were fantastic - but I'd only wanted to get to Brinscall! I had quite a long way to go after Brinscall and it was very, very hot. I trudged across the top of the moor for half an hour or so and then met somebody coming from the opposite direction. I asked whether or not Brinscall was just ahead, 'Well, no, not exactly' was the reply. As she said, I'd come 'the long way round', and there was still some distance to go. Bloody ramblers! Sure enough, after another age, there was the sign for the descent: Brinscall (Ramblers Association 1963), and at least another half an hour to get to the bottom. Then there followed several miles of road walking, crossing several major roads and creeping underneath the new M63 or 65 (can't remember which), before I finally reached Pleasington, exhausted, at about 4 o'clock.

No B&Bs on the way and no B&Bs in Pleasington where I'd hoped to stay. It was indeed pleasant (I'd chosen it specially on account of its name) and looked precisely the sort of place that would be brimming over with B&Bs. In the end I enquired in the Railway Inn, where the landlord said no, they didn't do B&B and he couldn't think of anywhere that did. I was hot, red and sweaty and he must have felt sorry for me because he then took over, while I sat on a bar stool with half a pint of shandy and chatted with his two fixtures. (Daytime pubs always seem to have two fixtures, one old and one young, boring the pants off each other - and the landlord as well as he stands polishing glasses behind the bar. You can almost hear him thinking, Oh God! Why don't they just go home? One thing though, fixtures are always glad to see you, even an oddball like me. They beam and smile over the introductions, 'I'm Mac ... Tom ... George ... pleashed to meet you. Isha lovely day for a stroll', etc.) The landlord was really nice, rang the Blackburn Tourist Information Centre, got the address of a B&B in Blackburn and offered to drive me there. He was marvellous; I would never have found the B&B on my own. It was on the outskirts of Blackburn, about two miles back the way I'd come and the address was just 'Pickerings', no number, in an endless road that had over

900 numbered houses. We had to call in at his friend the newsagent to ask where it was. Got there eventually and the proprietor was outside cutting down some trees. But in response to my request for B&B, he said he was sorry, he only had a single room vacant. I couldn't make out why I couldn't have it, and then the penny dropped: he thought my Railway Inn friend and I were a couple! So after clearing up the confusion I said goodbye to my kind Railway Inn friend and was then looked after by Peter of the B&B and *his* friend, the minister. I'd landed up in a Christian household! They were so nice but I was dying to get my boots off and have a shower. He had to get the room ready, he said, switch on the hot water. We had tea and cakes, then his wife came home, more chats, and finally, at about 6.30pm I was able to crash onto the bed. It's a pristine clean and well-designed modern house, which they built themselves nine years ago.

Feet bad: left foot now swollen, and painful on the arch and instep. I must have damaged it climbing up the blooming moors. Rash on my ankles too, due to the heat I suppose, plus another 14 (minimum) mile day.

These people are being really helpful and it's been decided that I'll stay here two nights, and Peter will fetch me back from Hurst Green tomorrow evening and drive me there again on Saturday morning. So generous and kind. It means I won't have to carry my pack for the day, so that will also help my foot get better.

Friday 30 April
Blackburn - Hurst Green

Set off once again for Pleasington, passing the Railway Inn on my way. I went on for miles after that without seeing a single B&B or even a hopeful pub, so it was lucky indeed that the friendly landlord had intervened the way he did. I've sent him a postcard of thanks. Left to my own devices I would almost certainly have trotted off, hoping for somewhere further along the way, but I was so tired by then, it would have been awful. Might even have been a silver bag job!

Anyway today was much better, no pack for a start. All the footpaths and bridleways worked out a treat and the first part was really beautiful; lovely feathery-leaved woods and open farmland. Masses of birds. I'm sure there is more bird life here than at home. Perhaps it's all the water.

Slight change in the route: I went via Mellor and side roads, then along a footpath to finally cross the River Ribble at Dinckley, over a swaying perilous little footbridge. The Ribble is beautiful, wide, fast flowing, quite shallow in parts where it washes over sparkling masses of smooth white stones. The sky was blue, the river was blue and I ate the delicious picnic that my landlady had insisted on giving me, lounging on the riverbank, boots off, under the shady trees with not a care in the world. My first proper picnic of the journey I think. I tend just to have a few snacky things, eating on the hoof as it were, either because I'm not hungry at midday after the big fried breakfasts, or because there's nowhere to sit, or it's raining. Or I haven't got any proper food anyway.

I went slowly today and tried to relax a bit. The last few days have been hectic, one way and another and I've been getting odd pains in my chest (once or twice the pain even radiated down my arm. Help!) This morning I requested scrambled eggs instead of my usual full fried breakfast, in case the chest pains are due to heart disease. Also, last night *both* my feet were really swollen, not just the bad foot. And because of the heat and the mileage they were also covered in rash. They looked a little bit like poor darling Jim's feet.

The morning's walk through those lovely dappled woods and then along the stretch of the River Ribble made me feel so much better. Went to bed very early again and ate the remains of my packed lunch in bed.

Saturday 1 May
Hurst Green (Dinckley) - Slaidburn

Peter and Stella have given me a cheque for £20 for the LRF. They've been so kind and thoughtful and I left there feeling genuinely fond of them both. I said I'd bring Berwyn next time and really felt we might keep in touch. Stella drove me to Dinckly again and we took her mother along too, just for the ride. They're a devoted family. Peter had tears in his eyes twice, once when I showed them Jim's picture (which I don't normally do, but it fell out when I was fishing around in my purse belt for something), and then again when I said goodbye. Kind, softhearted man with the bluff exterior. They were both maths teachers, retired early. They have two sons themselves. It could happen to any of us, is what people think. I read somewhere that pity and fear is a powerful combination, and I think that is true.

So off I went again from Dinckley, across the swaying suspension footbridge and past the unfriendly dogs the other side for the third and last time. Through Hurst Green and on to the Forest of Bowland, the place I've been looking forward to seeing since reading about it in the Wild Britain book at home. The day was hot and getting hotter. First part was lanes and a bit of riverside walking, the River Hodder now. By the afternoon I was avoiding short-cut footpaths because of losing the way briefly in the morning in a wooded part and having to scrabble down on my backside, difficult with a pack on. I've found that since the fall in Delamere Forest I'm a bit anxious on steep woody paths. My head must have healed, but it's still very sore to touch.

I had another picnic lunch given me by Stella, sitting on the banks of the River Hodder, feet dabbling in the water. I dallied there for an hour or so in the peace and tranquillity. Then through long lanes, climbing gently towards my Forest of Bowland. In the late afternoon there was a sudden dramatic change in the weather as I came over the brow of a hill. Clouds covered the sun and a chill wind blew, so that from being broiling hot, I was at first grateful for the coolth of the wind and then quickly became so cold I had to stop and put more clothes on. It was quite stark country up there, just moorland and tufts of yellow grass. Small belts of conifers. Not the Forest of Bowland proper yet, but I could see what I imagined was the Trough of Bowland in the distance.

Got to the youth hostel at about 6pm and it's very nice - the best yet and costs only £6.10 per night. Very friendly and there's carpet upstairs! There are lots of cyclists staying here and apparently this is a big cycling area.

Sunday 2 May
Day off; Slaidburn

Walked from Slaidburn to Dunsop Bridge (four miles) and back to reduce the number of miles I'll have to do tomorrow when Berwyn will be here. Can't wait to see him, it's three weeks since we last met. He's got lots of doctoring to do as well - head, back (the plaster Joanna put on to cover the grazes on my spine is still there), foot, heart.

The warden and his wife invited me in to the kitchen for tea so I could tell them all about the walk. Gosh! They were impressed and also quite envious. They were doing YH locum jobs all over the country and didn't know this area, and didn't know that Dunsop Bridge is supposed to be the exact centre of the British Isles. What's more, Bob, being a Yorkshireman brought up to believe that Yorkshire is the centre of the British Isles, refused to believe that it was! Intrigued, he went on a fact-finding mission to Dunsop Bridge to settle the matter and found that we were both right. Dunsop Bridge is the centre, but according to the old maps this part of Lancashire used to be Yorkshire! They were an interesting, friendly couple and even organised a whip round for me in aid of the LRF.

Monday 3 May
Slaidburn - Abbeystead

I sat on a bench in the village to wait for Berwyn who arrived at 10 o'clock just as he said he would! He'd left home at 4am and except for going round in circles near Clitheroe, he'd had an excellent journey. We drove off to Dunsop Bridge and I walked on to Abbeystead from there, whilst Berwyn went to find us a B&B for the next three nights. I had a lovely carefree walk: fields, lanes, chickens and little wooden bridges over streams. We met at Abbeystead and drove to Wharton, where Berwyn had booked us in to this very nice Free-Range Guest House. Or Home of Free Range, I think it's called. Oh the bliss of not having to concern myself about where I'm going to sleep and eat!

Today's walk went through the Trough of Bowland, quite steep, some of it, in the very heart of the area. Overall, the Forest of Bowland is lovely and I'm pleased I came here, but it wasn't quite as I'd imagined it would be. A lot of it is brown heather and grouse moor. And because it was a Bank holiday, there were hundreds of people picnicking on the measly bits of land at the side of the road, which is about the only place they're allowed to go. Tons of private notices, and despite the opening up of certain 'access areas' it certainly makes you realise you're in the midst of 'private land'. The Duke of Westminster owns it apparently, he who is richer than the Queen. All so a few stuffed aristocrats can feed on a meal that can't taste so very different from chicken.

Tuesday 4 May
Abbeystead - Caton

I changed today's route slightly to make it more direct and because the paths going over the 'access area' in the Forest of Bowland are apparently not well marked. Plus it didn't look very inviting. So, instead of going over the top of Clougha Pike into Crossgill and Liddlesdale, I kept on side roads to Quernmore and down into Caton. Easy day and parts of this walk were truly lovely, especially up on the moor near Abbeystead, where there were only farms, curlews and lapwings. I even saw some hares, and the last time I saw a hare was about 25 years ago in Dens Farm (near home).

Berwyn went into the city of Lancaster and did some sightseeing. He liked it a lot and visited the enormous building that dominates the Lancaster skyline, a Victorian mansion built to commemorate a city magnate of some renown and now a museum and gallery.

Wednesday 5 May
Caton - Warton

I had only a little journey from Caton to Wharton - a snip of a six-mile walk, so was back in the B&B by lunchtime. We shopped in Lancaster for Mam's[27] birthday tomorrow (she will be 96!) and then went on to see Morecambe, which was quite a funny place, all left over from the sixties with Victorian undertones. I was there once with Jackie Just[28] when I was about 15 years old. I remember we

---

27. Berwyn's mother, still living alone in her house in the Rhondda Valley, South Wales.
28. A friend from schooldays, with whom I have now lost touch.

spent the entire week and all our money on the slot machines, pausing only long enough to watch Petula Clark judging a bathing beauty parade.

It goes so quickly when Berwyn's here. We've had three whole days, gone in a flash.

Half-way in terms of TIME!

Thursday 6 May
Warton - Grange-over-Sands

Berwyn left for Wales. It's awful, again, saying goodbye to him. I miss him all the time, but it's most acute on the days when he goes. He's been such a love too, did the washing in the launderette, saw to all my ailments, ferried me to and fro to the next bit of walk, fed me, brought all the news, letters, photos, new package of maps. In addition this time, he listened to my plans for the new garden behind the barn, and (previously forewarned it has to be said) didn't scupper any of it! Designing that area is one of the things that's kept me going during the not-so-good days. Berwyn has full permission to blast away all the ideas, but only *after* I get home!

Finally and most importantly, he's decided to come next time when I most need him, before the long trek through the Drumochter Pass to Dalwhinnie. This means that I'll be pack-free and won't have to do the whole stretch in one go, a huge relief. I've been a bit bothered by the thought of that day. It would have been 19 miles, uphill all the way presumably, and I dare say it gets a bit airless in that massive pass. So that's a weight off my mind. And then we'll have a leisurely couple of days getting to Kingussie along the Spey Valley, which I've heard is lovely.

I feel a bit troubled by the fact that my walk has, and is, involving the time and attention of other people. I hadn't intended that. I'd thought I'd just go off and walk till I got there, and then Berwyn would come to take me home. But I seem to be needing quite a lot of his time and energy. He is really the one getting all the 'back-up system' organised, plus taking on the small worries regarding my health and fitness. I hadn't meant to worry him. And the boys have involved themselves too, worrying slightly and trying to think when they can come up and see me. They've all been so sweet, so loving - so necessary. All our friends too, Ellen and Colin[29] arrive on Sunday, and then Gill and Liz[30] who are driving hundreds of miles to Scotland and back just to accompany me for a few days. I do hope they'll enjoy it - and that I'll be able to get somewhere for us all to stay in the long B&B-less wastes of southern Scotland.

Today I walked via Silverdale to Arnside, and then took the little train over the viaduct across Morecambe Bay to Grange-over-Sands. I'd originally intended to visit the RSPB reserve at Leighton Moss, but I didn't have the energy, plus you need more time and better feet. So I was here quite early and am having a quiet time. Found a B&B easily and have also fixed one for tomorrow at the Tourist Information Centre. I was lucky to get this because everywhere is booked up to the hilt due to the arrival of a thousand orienteers, who are competing in the National Orienteering Championships this weekend. There were no vacancies at Spark Bridge where I'd hoped to stay, and so I'm going to Newby Bridge, only a few miles away.

Walked around this gentle little town and sat on a bench looking out over the miles of empty muddy sand. Heard the stories of people sinking in the sand, as televised recently on 999.

Friday 7 May
Grange over Sands - Newby Bridge.

Slept for 11 hours last night and feel better today. I felt terribly tired all of yesterday, don't know why, because I hadn't had big days. I've been shifting things around in my pack and altering the way I walk, in an effort to eradicate the pain in my left side, which was so bad yesterday. I'm sure it is muscular, or root pain from the spine, as Berwyn suggested. Not heart anyway. And it was better today. Maybe I was walking in too upright a position (I'd adopted this stance in order to prevent the pack rubbing on my spine). Posture - that's the thing!

I went via Cartmel, a beautiful village just outside the Lake District National Park, and the inhabitants want to know why this

---

29. Ellen and Colin Inman. Our friends for many years, living in Wadhurst.
30. Gill James and Liz Kittermaster. Friends of many years, living in the Wadhurst area.

is? They feel quite strongly that they should be within the national park border. Saw my first tourist bus there and I expect there'll be lots more from now on. I kept to the lanes and eschewed all footpaths a) because it's very wet and b) because I couldn't bear the thought of ending up lost or in a block end and having to retrace my steps.

It's odd, at the beginning of the walk I expected that my level of fitness would increase all the time, so that by now I should be positively bursting with muscle and strength. But I seem to have reached a plateau, and am still often tired and aching at the end of a day. Today for example, was only seven miles and not too hilly, but I was so pleased to get here and get my boots off. It's going to be much steeper in the Lake District proper, and as for Scotland....

Had so many thoughts when I was walking today, but now they've all dissipated. I was writing to Jim, another letter like I've done at home. And I was thinking about pain, mental and physical. I've never forgotten the sudden realization I had years ago, a few days after Dad died[31], that the agony of mental pain is far worse than mere physical pain. Mainly because you can do something about physical pain, escape is possible even if only temporarily. Mental anguish is indestructible and you do not know how you can bear it. And so I was thinking about Jim, and the nightmare for him of experiencing both kinds of pain and for all that time. He was so incredibly brave. Sometimes I knew he wanted painkillers when the physical pain probably didn't warrant the amount. It did often, but not always. But who could blame him wanting to obliterate the mental pain as well, all the misery of it, and only he to bear it - alone. Isolated in it.

He never once said 'why me?' - the cry of so many. As he said at the beginning, talking about the man in the next bed who'd been asking that question, 'Why *not* him?' He was irritated that the man seemed outraged that something different had happened to him. Was he so much of a sheep, Jim wanted to know, that he only ever wanted even the same health as everyone else? But Jim was so aware of what was happening, so completely au fait with all the details of his illness, the limitations of the treatment, the reasons why they were unable to treat certain aspects of the disease, the dashed hopes,

---

31. My father died of acute myeloid leukaemia, aged 63 years.

the futile attempts to improve his general health, the improvement in one area always countered with a flare up of trouble or crisis in another. Day after day, week after week, for 15 weeks. I never cease to think how brave he was. I've never in my life, nursing days included, encountered such resilience, fortitude, courage, strength of mind.

Saturday 8 May
Newby Bridge - Coniston

A long day and raining for most of it. It was to have been a 10-mile journey from Spark Bridge, but because of having a B&B at Newby Bridge it was a longer day - 15 miles. It was a lovely walk however, despite the rain. The first part was along lanes bordered by woods. The beeches are now just out, clad in their feathery light green. Lakeland villages are quite pretty, but the dark stone gives them a rather gaunt and severe look, especially in the pouring rain. Crossed to the other side of Lake Coniston over a bridge at the bottom, and there was the Lake, stretched out before me in all its glory. Walked a bit of the main road to reach Sunny Bank, where I joined the Cumbria Way[32], the long-distance path that will take me all the way to Carlisle. At this section the path follows the banks of Lake Coniston into town, a distance of 3.75 miles according to the book, and it certainly felt like it, lovely though it was, and the going was easy.

The area is full of recreational people, not only the Championship orienteers. On the eastern side of Lake Coniston there were 1400 walkers doing the annual walk from Keswick to Barrow-in-Furness, a distance of 40 miles. I met them in dribs and drabs all the way, and there was the much-repeated witticism that I was going in the wrong direction! Further along, Lake Coniston was alive with people in boats of all description.

Had a much-needed pot of tea and toasted cheese when I arrived in Coniston and got to the YH on the dot of 5pm. Ellen and Colin arrived around 6.30pm and we had a very merry meeting upstairs in my 12-bedded girls' dorm. They were booked in to a B&B down the road. It was great to see them again and we went out into the sheeting rain to have supper in a big spacious pub, choc-a-bloc full of walkers.

---

32. *The Cumbria Way & The Allendale Ramble*, by Jim Watson. A Cicerone Guide, 1997.

Sunday 9 May
Coniston - Dungeon Ghyll

The predicted 13-mile walk according to the book turned out to be only 10 and a half by our reckoning, so it was quite an easy day. There were lots of people at Tarn Hows, a famous beauty spot, but hardly a soul at Elterwater a bit further on and much more beautiful. A pair of swans, swimming leisurely at the water's edge, crooking their necks and bowing to each other, put the finishing touches to this idyllic place. We followed the Cumbria Way, now getting progressively more mountainous, as far as Dungeon Ghyll, where Colin had booked us all in to the Old Dungeon Ghyll Hotel, a solid, good, old-fashioned place. Colin went back to Coniston by bus to fetch the car and my pack. We had dinner in the restaurant and I felt thoroughly spoilt; easy day, no pack, no map-reading and B&B all booked!

Heard all the news from Wadhurst and it was great to catch up on everything.

Monday 10 May
Day off; Dungeon Ghyll

After a leisurely breakfast we moseyed up to the Tarn at the top of Pavey Ark. That took a while and the weather was a bit rainy and cold, but it wasn't too strenuous. Marvellous views of the lakes and fells from the top. We sat a while and watched the daring people traverse Jack's Rake, a precipitous climb through a crack in the rocks of Pavey Ark. I can't begin to imagine what it must be like to feel drawn to these uninviting climbs! Ellen would have liked to have a stab at it though. Trouble was, there was nobody willing to accompany her in the enterprise. I wish I were more intrepid.

Back in the hotel, Ellen cut my hair for me! Bless her heart; she'd come prepared with scissors having guessed that her services might be required. And she did a wonderful job, it looks great and feels so much better. It's weeks since it was last cut and I've been looking more and more like an Old English sheepdog. I'd planned to get it done in the great metropolitan areas around Manchester, but when I was there I couldn't bear the thought of it because of my poor sore head.

Tuesday 11 May
Dungeon Ghyll - Stonethwaite

On our way again along the Cumbria Way, but this time according to plan B, in which Colin drove the car ahead to Keswick and then back to find us a B&B in Stonethwaite. Once again I wouldn't have to carry my pack. Outside it was absolutely teeming with rain and had been doing so throughout the night. Because of the teeming, pouring, cloudbursts of rain, Ellen and I put off setting out till about 10.30am in the hope that the deluge would abate, but no. There were occasional cracks in the massing clouds overhead but it only ever stopped long enough for it to be termed 'raining' rather than 'downpour'. Quite early on, Ellen slipped on a boulder whilst crossing one of the many swollen streams, and came crashing down on her face. She bruised her nose (we hoped it wasn't broken) and cut her lip. It clearly shook her up a bit but no real damage was done and she wouldn't hear of turning back. It got better, although her face swelled up more and more throughout the day as we continued on our sopping way through Stake Pass and beyond. At the top of the Pass we couldn't cross the stream because it had turned into a gushing, torrenting river, making its way full tilt for the waterfall we'd just come up by. In the end we had to make what was for me, a nerve-racking leap from a slippery wet boulder at the edge of the 'stream'. Ellen didn't give it another thought, mountain goat that she is! The rain continued and my boots let in so much water I could feel it sloshing around under my socks. We stopped briefly for some lunch, sitting on a rock that protected us from the worst of the weather, and then continued on our soggy, craggy way, mostly downhill, sploshing through streams, torrents and runnels of water.

We met Colin half way down to Langstrath and he was a bit taken aback at the sight of Ellen's poor bruised face! The waterfall at Langstrath was spectacular and the rain stopped long enough for us to take photos. Then on our way again, along the wide valley bottom, quite barren here, bereft of vegetation except for the odd clump of gorse, and the river running through the middle. Ellen is in her element in the hills, and would have happily stayed up there longer! But I was thankful to arrive in Stonethwaite, the day having confirmed that for me, mountains are not the special place they are for so many people.

Stonethwaite is a lovely village and Colin had found us a very snug B&B. We dried out, had hot baths and drove to near-by Rosthwaite for supper. More great parties of walkers, Rosthwaite being on the Coast to Coast path as well as the Cumbria Way.

Wednesday 12 May
Stonethwaite - Keswick

A good quick walk to Keswick, where we had the choice of a million B&Bs. We also got various jobs done: specs mended, shopping and I also had my boots re-heeled - just in the nick of time too. They were down to the next layer of material and apparently I'd have walked through that in no time at all, then it would have been a question of new boots. I'm a bit disappointed in my boots, comfortable though they are. I hadn't expected them to go through so quickly and they are certainly not waterproof. A nice girl in the Mister Minute cobblers mended them for me, free of charge. Keswick must be the best place in the whole of Britain to get walking boots repaired. It's also an attractive town but probably gets pretty awful in the holiday season when it's full. Virtually every house in our road is a B&B establishment and all the shops are geared towards walkers, climbers and other leisure activities. Gorgeous cake shop and lots of eating places.

Thursday 13 May
Keswick - Orthwaite

We had quite a steep walk up to Skiddaw this morning and then were surrounded by eyefulls of wide sweeping fells and wonderful colours, browns, russet-red, yellows and green. We had our picnic lunch sitting on a bench outside Skiddaw House youth hostel, the highest and probably the loneliest hostel in Britain, where nobody is ever turned away. Just a few sheep to share the panoramic views over this wild and spartan landscape. Then a lovely walk 'back of Skiddaw' took us to Orthwaite, where Colin, in his inimitable fashion, had parked the car that morning. We drove back to Keswick for a second night there, taking the scenic route so that we had yet more splendid views of the Lake District. It's as beautiful as they say, and the good thing is that, despite its popularity, in the places where we were walking there was hardly anybody about.

Friday 14 May
Orthwaite - Caldbeck

We set off from Keswick for the last time to just outside Orthwaite where we'd got permission to leave the car for the day. This last day's walk with Ellen and Colin was lovely and different again, this time through gentle, pastoral country, not steep, heading north out of the Lake District. We saw a lamb being born in a field, and many others being herded, tended and transported here and there. It was a day of tranquillity, and we stretched out on a bank, eating and snoozing in the warm sunshine.

We arrived in the village of Caldbeck during the late afternoon, which has just about everything a village should have: village green, ducks on the pond, river running alongside the quiet back lane (just outside our B&B), historic old church and even a famous grave in the churchyard - John Peel.

Colin took a taxi ride back to fetch the car and the kindly driver refused the fare when he heard about my walk, so Colin donated it to the LRF. Then we had an excellent home-cooked meal in the old country pub that sits, of course, in the middle of this classically equipped village.

Saturday 15 May
Caldbeck - Carlisle

Said goodbye to Ellen and Colin on the banks of the Cald Beck outside the old churchyard. I'll miss them, they've been such great company, as well as doing so much in the way of map reading and organizing things so I didn't have to carry my pack. It's strange to think that they'll shortly be back in Wadhurst and getting on with a normal life there. For my part though, it feels as though I'm the one who'll be going back to normal life. Beginning each day with the morning's routine: filling up water bottles, packing up my belongings, every item placed meticulously in its usual position in the pack or in the pockets outside (army-style I expect, everything in its place!), the final check for the three separate and crucial items: purse belt, map-case, stick. Then payings and goodbyes, and off I go again, plodding along, thinking of this and that, mostly Jim-a-long today, aware of trees, birds, the landscape in general. It's a funny thing, this feeling that normality is this *now*, this quiet, daily trudge all on my own, into the unknown. And I am never lonely, never afraid.

This was the last day of the Cumbria Way, which has been altogether a very good long-distance path. Today it was through lovely countryside, woods at first and then following the River Caldew all the way. I went wrong once, on the outskirts of Carlisle, but picked the path up again after a bit of wandering and then it took me almost to the centre of Carlisle. Which looks a very attractive town, the bits I saw of it. Sadly I didn't have enough energy to visit the famous cathedral. It was a 15-mile walk (excluding when I got lost) then more miles and considerable time spent milling around the town centre, trying to find the B&B. Nobody seemed to have heard of the street it was in, and I only had half a map. The B&B was recommended to me by someone I'd met in Coniston YH and I had it all booked. Even more crucially, my pack was waiting there for me! Ellen and Colin's last act of kindness was to drive it to the B&B this morning, on their way home. Found it in the end of course, and there was my backpack, safely installed in my room.

All our friends have been absolutely superb during the time of Jim's illness and afterwards. And look at them, still at it. Ellen and Colin, so sensitive and supportive and loving. They have walked many miles, Ellen with a sore face, broken tooth and a blistered foot, Colin, rushing around, organizing, collecting the car to save me carrying the pack. They are friends indeed.

Had a meal in the Bee Hive at my landlady's suggestion. When I got back she was waiting for me in the hall, full of questions. What did I have to eat, how much did it cost, why was I doing the journey, what was it for? She's nice, Irish, and suggests that God takes the good people first. My room is about four floors up, with a bathroom next-door housing a nightmare of a shower. It runs between scalding hot and nearly cold regardless of how carefully you manipulate the taps.

Tomorrow is another long day and for the first time will be all along an A road. The distance to Canonbie, the only place I could get B&B, is too far for me to make detours along lanes or B roads. And it had to be fixed because I'm meeting Gill and Liz there. The last of my visitors.

Today is the end of Stage III and tomorrow will be my last day in England! Who would have thought that Scotland is so big as to take up two fifths of the journey?

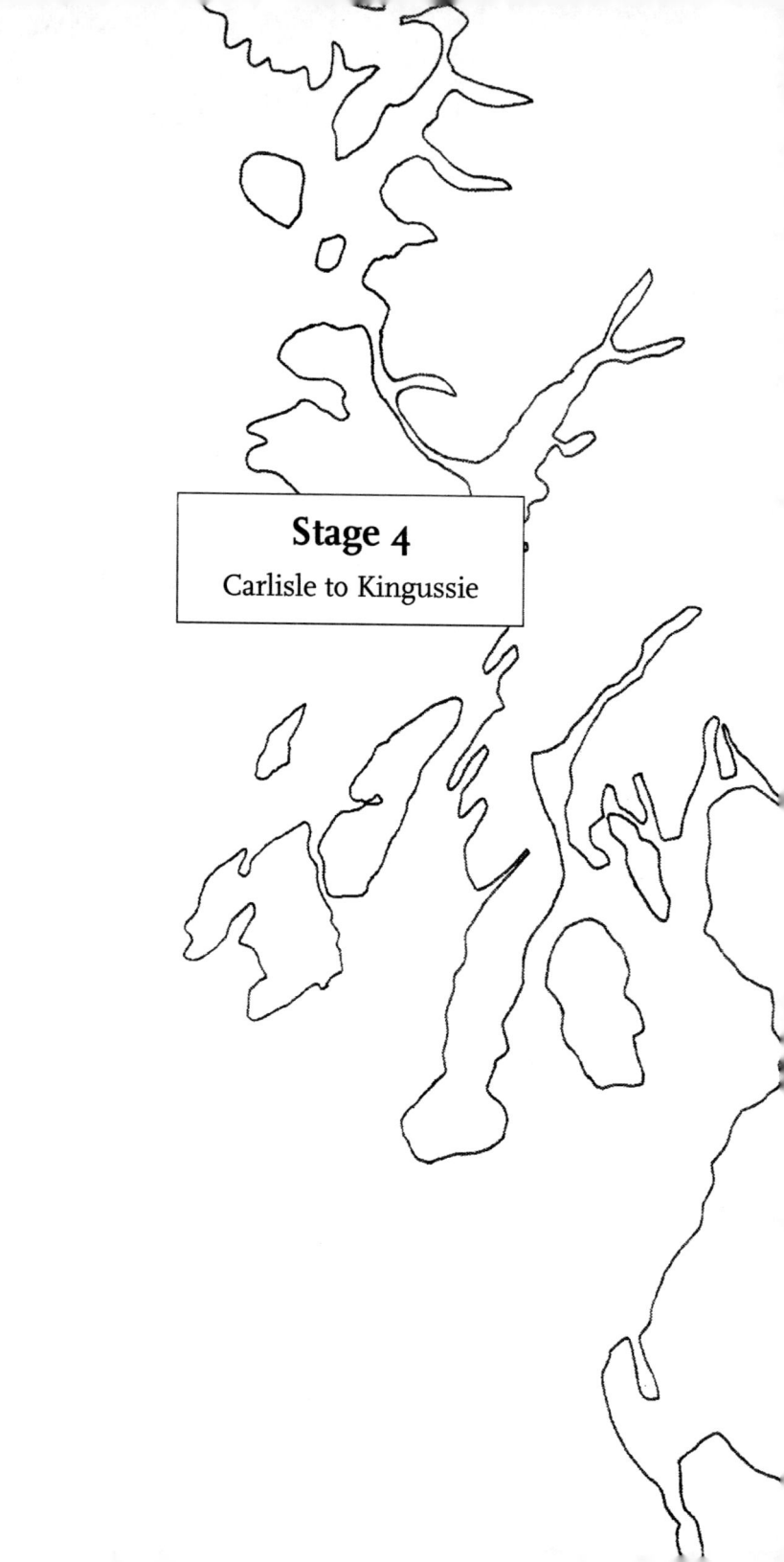

Stage 4
Carlisle to Kingussie

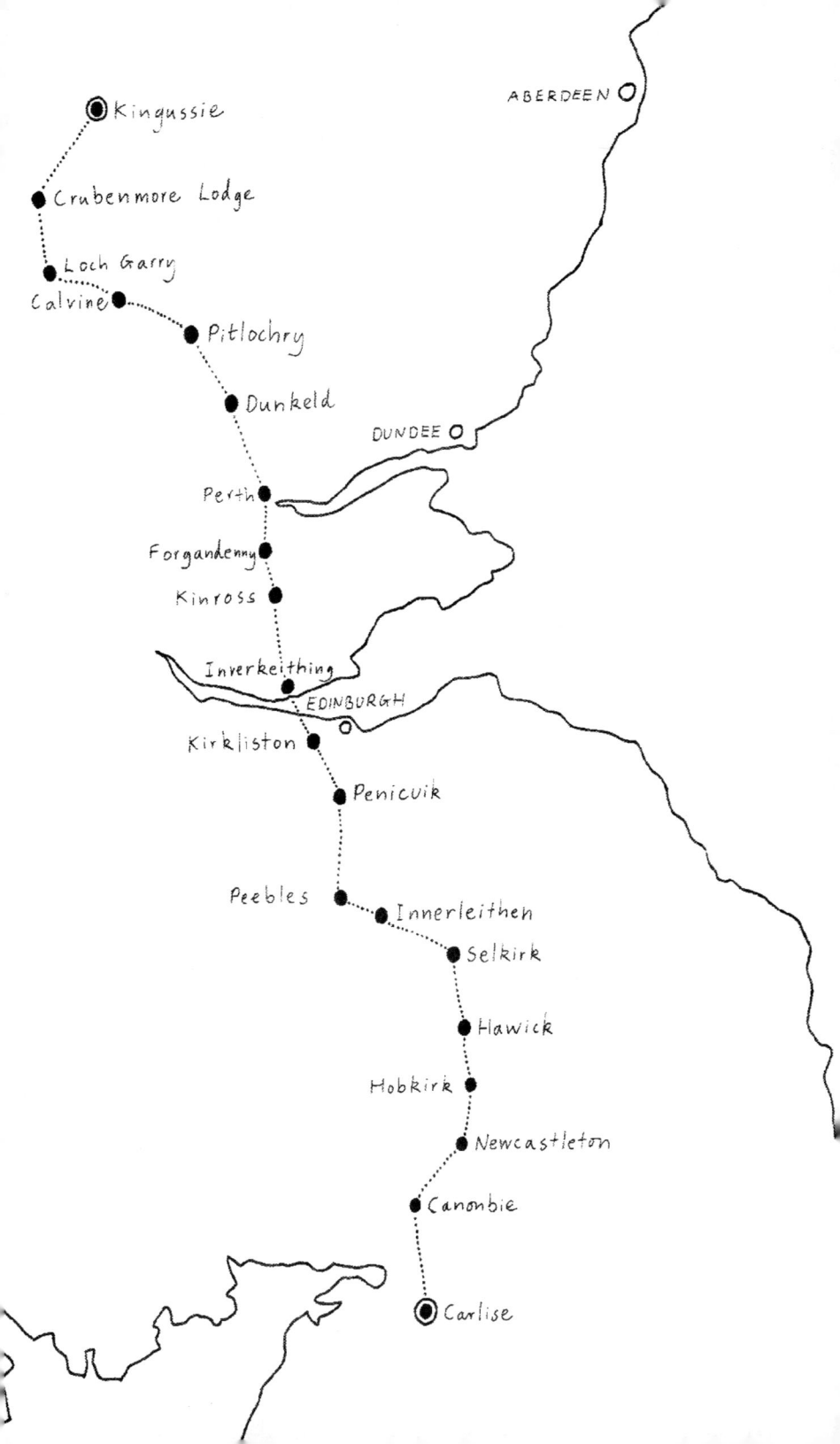

- Kingussie
- Crubenmore Lodge
- Loch Garry
- Calvine
- Pitlochry
- Dunkeld
- ABERDEEN
- DUNDEE
- Perth
- Forgandenny
- Kinross
- Inverkeithing
- EDINBURGH
- Kirkliston
- Penicuik
- Peebles
- Innerleithen
- Selkirk
- Hawick
- Hobkirk
- Newcastleton
- Canonbie
- Carlise

Carlisle to Kingussie

Borders - Pentland Hills - Ochil Hills - Drumochter Pass
Sunday, 16 May - Friday, 4 June

OS 85 Carlisle

Carlisle, A7, Longtown, **Canonbie**.	14 miles

OS 85 + 79 Hawick

Canonbie, Rowanburn, **Newcastleton**.	17 miles

OS 79 + 80 Cheviot Hills

Newcastleton, Dinlabyre, **Hobkirk**.	14 miles
Hobkirk, Hawick.	10 miles

OS 79 + 73 Peebles

Hawick, Drinkstone Hill, Synton Mossend, Ashkirk, Hartwoodburn, **Selkirk**.	12 miles
Selkirk, *Southern Upland Way* to Three Brethren, Traquair, **Innerleithen**.	13 miles
Innerleithen, Peebles.	7 miles

OS 73 + 66 Edinburgh

Peebles, Leadburn **Penicuik**.	14 miles

OS 66 + 65 Falkirk

Penicuik, Mauricewood, Pentland Hills, Balerno, Currie, Ratho, **Kirkliston**. 17 miles

Kirkliston, Queensferry, Forth Bridge, **Inverkeithing**. 7 miles

OS 65 + 58 Perth

Inverkeithing, Hill of Beath, Keltybridge, Gairney Bank, **Kinross**. 12 miles

Kinross, Milnathort, Middleton, Pathstruie, Craighall, **Forgandenny**. 16 miles

Forgandenny, Forteviot, Aberdalgie, **Perth**. 8 miles

OS 58 + 53 Blairgowrie

Perth, Luncarty, Bankfoot, Waterloo, Birnam, **Dunkeld**. 17 miles

Dunkeld, Inver, Dalguise, Balnamuir, Tay bridge, Logierait, Dunfallandy, **Pitlochry**. 13 miles

OS 43 Blair Atholl

Pitlochry, Killiekrankie, Blair Atholl, **Calvine**. 12 miles

OS 42 Glen Garry

Calvine, General Wade's Military Road, **Loch Garry**. 13 miles

OS 42 + 35 Kingussie

Loch Garry, Drumochter Pass, Dalwhinnie, **Crubenmore Lodge**. 12 miles

Crubenmore Lodge, Spey bridge, Newtonmore, **Kingussie**. 9 miles

Total **237 miles**

(19 days walking, average 12.5 miles per day. Days off: 1)

In the Ochil Hills.

Stage IV

Sunday 16 May
Carlisle - Canonbie

Through the quiet of the Sunday morning town and then straight up the A7. At least there was pavement for four miles, and not too much traffic after a point where several main roads branched off east and west. It was the first day of walking entirely along a main road and wasn't as bad as I'd expected, though it did seem long. Longtown (aptly named I thought) was halfway, and I was sitting eating crisps, Twiglets and Turkish Delight by the wide and beautiful River Eske when a decrepit and drunken Irishman came and sat on the bench beside me. He ruined the peace by talking incessantly at me, all about his fishing exploits and near-drowning experiences, and though he was amusing I could see he was never going to move on, so I did. He followed me for a while until my pace outdid his!

I crossed the border into Scotland just before Canonbie. Scotland Welcomes You, the notice said and the B&B at Canonbie certainly did. A thoroughly welcoming landlady ushered me into an ultra-frilly, satin-covered, twin-bedded room, which had a chair converting to a third bed. Gill and Liz arrived about an hour later, having driven all the way from Sussex. We greeted each other with gusto and within minutes the neat room was transformed to a homely state of chaos! They'd brought champagne, little eats, and all the photos of Matt and Loshana's wedding[33], so we made merry and I heard all the gossip. They were full of fun and enthusiasm for the journey, and I was hoping the days wouldn't be too long for them, tomorrow especially, as the only B&B I could find is some three miles further on after the village of Newcastleton. Also the next two days are going to be all road-walking, albeit small roads.

---

33. Matthew James (Gill's son) and Loshana, his wife.

Monday 17 May
Canonbie - Newcastleton

It was long. Not quite sure how long because there was a discrepancy between the mileage as counted on the milometer of Liz's car next day when Gill retraced our steps in it, and the mileage as calculated from my map wheelie. It's a conundrum. Anyway, it was either 16.5 (my reckoning) or 18.2 (Gill's reckoning), so I've logged it in as 17 miles. And except for a three or four mile section along a disused railway line and a forest path (where we were lost for a while) it was hard road all the way. Nice country, if a bit foresty, and not too hilly. There were occasional convoys of very fast log lorries that, we learned later from our landlady, will be an increasing problem in the next few years. By then the vast plantations in the Kielder Forest will have reached their harvesting time, and the local population is wondering how this narrow, quiet B road, which is the only transport route available, will cope with hundreds of these dangerous lorries thundering along every day. There is a strong movement to re-open the railway but this is opposed by about half of the landowners because it would be expensive, plus a lot of the line and some stations have been built over. Poor things, I certainly wouldn't want to live near that road in five years time.

Our B&B was called Borders Honey Farm and was surrounded by forest. As is so often the case, there was no name at the roadside and we'd gone half a mile up the forest track before we knew for sure we'd arrived at the right place. So we arrived in an exhausted heap, but revived quite quickly in the splendour of our surroundings and fortified by quantities of tea and cake. It was a luxury B&B, everything you could wish for in terms of extras: lotions and potions in the bathroom, biscuits in the bedrooms, the use of the magnificent sitting room, tankfulls of scalding hot water and a deep, deep bath. It was owned by a couple from Kent, who had renovated and extended the house during the four years they'd had it, transforming it from a tumbledown wreck to its present very smart state. We saw all the pictures. We tossed a coin for the second bedroom with its big double bed and Gill won. Her foot was getting more painful and she had clearly felt the miles. I had too, and had painful soles of feet, probably because the big new heels on my boots tip me forward so. Liz was tired but OK.

Tuesday 18 May
Newcastleton - Hobkirk

This morning Gill's feet were worse and she'd had a bad night. It was decided she'd ask our landlady to give her a lift back to Canonbie to fetch the car and have the day off so as not to worsen the situation. This had the added advantage of having the car nearer to us if it was needed. So that is what we did.

Liz and I stepped out along the quiet, scenic road leading to Hobkirk, forested hills stretching up steeply on one side of the road, stream rippling through low hills on the other. We talked about Dick[34] and about Jim. She's very sweet and I feel so sorry for her; she's most courageous. We'd stopped for a break and were bathing our feet in the icy cold stream when, with expert timing, Gill rounded the corner in the car. We dawdled there for some time, and altogether had an easier day.

Our B&B is in the lovely dappelly valley of Hobkirk. The house, which used to be The Manse, is one of only a handful of houses set in the in the midst of beautiful beeches, with a river along the way and small undulating hills surrounding the whole secret place. Gill had a fearful job finding the place in the car, so it was lucky for Liz and me that she'd gone on ahead and then walked out to meet us and guide us in. We're about seven miles from Hawick, one and a half from Bonchester Bridge. This was a bit of a detour from the original route because of the dearth of B&Bs. This place and tomorrow's B&B were eventually found and booked by Gill before she left home.

It's all very smart and clean, and tonight I won the toss and have the room to myself. Lovely bed with thick white cotton sheets and duvet cover, big room and I've even washed my nightie. Our landlady is an upright Scottish lady, sweet but very serious. We all got the giggles at supper-time, for no real reason except that when everything is so very solemn and tidy it makes you feel nervous. We had to ring a little bell at the end of each course to let her know we'd finished. In the first place nobody liked to ring the bell, and then when one of us had sufficiently braced herself to ring, the other two would collapse into convulsive laughter! We soon reached the state

---

34. Dick Kittermaster. Liz's husband, who died only a short while after Jim.

when the slightest incident was enough to trigger off more giggles, and we think we may have disgraced ourselves. Anyway it was a good meal, three courses and a glass of wine included in the deal for £10 a head.

Wednesday 19 May
Hobkirk - Hawick

Today's walk was about 10 miles we think; no map for the first bit because Hobkirk and its environs is off my original route. Another lovely day and we had long breaks for snacks and foot bathings in the wee burn. It's beautiful country. Gill's feet are OK now. Gill and Liz each drove the car halfway and then left it in the massive Hawick car park. We looked in a wool factory-shop and they both bought jumpers. Then off to find our B&B which was about two miles west of Hawick (pronounced Hoik) and seemed longer. Felt tired today. Our landlady fed us, which was great, as we didn't have to return to the town to get a meal. We had a slightly difficult time looking at her Cashmere shop because nearly everything was horrid. However, Liz managed to find a pink jumper and scarf, so that let Gill and me off the hook.

Thursday 20 May
Hawick - Selkirk

Today was another lovely day, warm sunshine and clear blue skies. We're having the best weather in the whole country apparently. Scenic walk across the hills from the B&B for the first five miles, through a forest plantation where we made a few mistakes, and then a further two or three miles of main road (A7). Ended with another easy stretch through forest and farmland, before dropping into Selkirk, an attractive, small town. David Steele lives here. Our B&B was in the centre and we had a good blow-out at the Cross Keys. We heard all about Fletcher, the only man returning from Flodden Field in 1513, and the gathering of 1400 horses on June 18 every year, processing through the main street of Selkirk.

Friday 21 May
Selkirk - Innerleithen

Saw Liz and Gill off onto their bus in the Market Place at 9.40am. They looked merry and brown from all the sun and I think had really enjoyed themselves. I certainly had. Gill's foot was none the worse for the hard walking, and Liz had only suffered a few pains in her hips. They were marvellous company, so bright and cheery and full of fun.

So while they went off on the long journey back to Sussex, I set out on my Southern Uplands day. I'd reverted to my original plan of going over the hills to Innerleithen via the Southern Upland Way, on the recommendation of our landlord, who said it was so glorious up there and not difficult from Selkirk. He gave me good directions and it was easy to find my way up to the Three Brethren and from there it was just a question of following the Southern Upland Way path, well-trodden and way-marked at every point.

BUT - THERE WAS A CHANGE IN THE WEATHER! From the fine drizzle with which the day began, it was blowing a gale-force wind and pouring with rain by the time I was only half way up to the top. I was battling to keep upright from then on. The wind and horizontal rain was belting in from the west, a sideways blast on my way up to the ridge, which became head on once I was on the top and walking in a westerly direction. All the way it pushed and buffeted me and I had a job to advance at all some of the time. The wind came in great gusts, of up to 70mph according to the TV news I saw later. The rain turned to sleet and for about half an hour, when I was approaching the Three Brethren, it was sheer hell. Every footstep was a struggle and I was seriously beginning to think I might never get any further. In the distance was a huge forest and though I normally dislike dark forest walks, it now became my idea of a haven, if only I could reach it. At one point the rain stopped and the sun came out fleetingly between wild scudding clouds, so I was able to glimpse the view, dark and hazy but clear enough to picture how spectacular it would be on a fine day. I was particularly taking note of the panorama to the north, range upon range of hills as far as the eye could see, and wondering how I'll get through all that lot. A bit of a challenge.

I finally reached the relative shelter of the forest but by then it was very cold. I trudged through the forest to the last peak, Minchmore, not bothering with the viewing-point as the weather had closed in again by then. On the lower slopes of the final descent into Innerleithen I was interested to see my first bothy, complete with Scotsman inside! Bothys are erected for the safety and comfort of long-distance walkers and climbers and I was approaching it to see what it was like inside when I saw a pair of knees through the open door. They belonged to a young Scotsman who had come the same way as me but from further off - he started out from Galashiels. He was soaked to the skin and said how dreadful the weather had been, which somehow made me feel better. He was resting and drying his clothes. I didn't see the inside of the bothy after all, but it looked quite cosy from the glimpse I had.

Happily I had my B&B at Innerleithen booked, so all I had to do was stagger, dripping, into the St Ronan's Hotel on the High Street. Very nice. £20.

Days like today certainly make you aware of the crucial importance of having the right gear. Notes on gear:

Clothes: although my outside was completely drenched, at no point did I get wet inside. The Paramo trousers were so sodden-looking it was unbelievable that my legs were dry, but they were. The only problem in terms of clothes was the cold, and that was my fault. I should have put on my long-sleeved T-shirt this morning, or at least stopped to put on gloves. My hands were numb with cold. But today's experience taught me a lesson: if you're walking into the teeth of the gale, every step a struggle and every nut, bolt and fibre of your body focused on keeping going, to make yourself stop even for a moment is just too great a psychological turn-about. Even though the outcome would be so beneficial in terms of warmth and comfort. Resolution: wrap up more *before* the going gets tough.

Backpack: the mackintosh cover kept my pack beautifully dry and I even stopped once to make sure this essential item wasn't in danger of blowing away. The mackintosh cover was one of Shally and Richard's useful tips, explaining that a wet pack is very much heavier than a dry one, so better to keep the things dry from the outside, rather than merely covering the contents with plastic.

Stick: marvellous company as usual. I never cease being grateful to Chris[35] for making it for me. It's one of the three items I feel have been absolutely essential for comfort (the other two being the Paramo trousers and the mackintosh pack cover). Originally I'd thought a stick would be good to have as an extension to my arm, to wave about and make me feel braver if confronted by dogs. But it's been absolutely invaluable in so many other ways: heaving me up hills, steadying me going downhill or when it's slippery, testing the depths of water and bog, clearing brambles and leaning on when I'm tired. Happily, I haven't yet had occasion to put it to its original use - so far, that is.

Boots: my boots are very comfortable and good on slippery ground. But they do let in the water and they're not supposed to. Perhaps I haven't treated them with enough stuff.

Saturday 22 May
Innerleithen - Peebles

At breakfast there were three 'proper' walkers in beards and shorts, who were doing the 210 miles of the Southern Upland Way in two weeks. They were talking about yesterday's weather, and one of them claimed that never in all his walking years, had he experienced such ferocious wind and rain! So that made me feel better too, especially as they were travelling in an easterly direction and therefore had had the wind behind them, whereas I had been walking due west straight into it. They were astonished that I was walking alone (the usual) and were 'very pleased indeed' to meet me! The wild weather was also on the news last night, 60 - 70 mph gusts reported and in the north (Aviemore) they'd had snow. It's unbelievable when I think how warm and summery it was when Gill and Liz were here the day before yesterday.

Today was similar, rain and a strong wind but not so rough. I only had to do a seven-mile, low-level walk, mostly road, but beginning with a lovely stretch along the banks of the River Tweed. The landlord had advised me against the quieter B road because of all the works traffic from the construction of a new golf course - at least I think that's what he said! I'm having real difficulty with Scottish

---

35. Chris Velten. Our friend and neighbour, who made Stick for me to take on the walk.

accents. In this morning's conversation with my landlord I got about one word in three and sometimes only the last word in a sentence.

The approach into Peebles, again along the River Tweed, was very inviting. Peebles itself is a gentle, peaceful sort of place. Full of little old, privately-owned shops and not a chain store in sight. The very efficient Tourist Information people had got me a B&B within minutes and by 1pm I'd booked in with Mrs Muir, changed my clothes and was back in town again for lunch. Found a nice wee place just off the High Street.

Tomorrow I'm going on a new route, not up through the hills McCloy-style as planned, because it really kills me in weather like this. So I've had to buy another map (Edinburgh) and I'm going due north on what I hope will be a good path along the disused railway line not far from the A road to Penicuik. From there I'll cross the Pentland Hills to Balerno next day and on as planned.

In addition to planning this new route, I've been to the bank, shopped, done the washing, phoned Berwyn and Mam, written four postcards and an airmail letter. I've had a bath, shaved my legs, cut my toe nails, creamed my feet, caught up to date with this diary, sorted my pack, eaten a salmon tartlet and now is my reward: good book and a long read in bed!

Just to add: the boys and Tam, Philip, Jo, Willie, Patrick, Eva and David G[36]. will all be on their way across the Channel now. They were booked on the 8 o'clock boat from Portsmouth to begin their weeks cycle trip to France. Hope they're careful. Only Berwyn left in England now.

Sunday 23 May
Peebles - Penicuik

Not a very nice day. I never managed to get to the dismantled railway (private notices and/or parts of it too overgrown or non-existent) so did the whole 14 miles along the dead straight A road. It was still very windy so it's a good thing I didn't go over the hills (don't want to repeat the day before yesterday).

Pain in chest most of the day, same as I had before. I'm sure it's to do with carrying the pack. I tried to keep my arms forward and

---

36. The boys & Tam; Philip (the boys' cousin), Jo (Dan's girlfriend), Willie, Eva (Jim's friends), Patrick, Dave (Michael's friends).

hunch a bit, ape-like. The pain never really went though. Sore throat too, so when I finally got myself a room I dosed myself with aspirin. Had an awful job getting anywhere, there were no B&Bs at all and it's quite a big town. I'd passed the Royal Hotel on my way in and disregarded it because of probable cost. I then traipsed around for about an hour and even went to the Highland Games that were being held in the park - bagpipes, swirling kilts and hammers being thrown about, but nobody knew of a B&B. I'd been directed there by a kind soul who thought the St John's ambulance might be able to help. About three people recommended the Royal and this is where I ended up. Not a bad place, but £30.

I go across the Pentland Hills in the morning and then I hope to find somewhere in the Balerno area for the last night before crossing the Firth of Forth.

I feel much less confident about directions and precisely where I am in Scotland. I look at the map on the TV weather forecast for the brief moment it's shown, and sometimes am pushed to know my exact whereabouts. In England I always knew. I'm becoming a bit more familiar with the Scottish outline though, I zoom in on the deep clefty bit around Edinburgh and go from there. I like having a TV in the room, mainly for the news (and Corrers of course).

I got fed up with Scotland today though; 'All mountains and main roads' I was grumbling to myself! There's no doubt, walking along a main road does nothing for your appreciation of the surrounding countryside. That, and the wind, and the background pain in my chest kept me from 'enjoying', as they say.

Local TV *Reporting Scotland*

Monday 24 May
Penicuik - Kirkliston

Actually written on Tuesday. By the time I got to Kirkliston all I was fit for was bath, sock-wash and bed. The morning was great, over the Pentland Hills from Mauricewood to Balerno. I loved the Pentland Hills, rolling, not too steep and covered in great clumps of sweet-smelling, bright yellow gorse. Only met two other walkers and the views from the top were fantastic. The path was easy to follow, and the way up to the Pentlands went through wooded bits that comprised my two favourite trees: tall Scots pine and beech trees just coming into leaf. Can't get better than that. It was quite windy, and on the reservoir there were two families of geese traversing the very choppy waters. One family was led by an adult, followed by seven goslings and the other parent bringing up the rear, sandwich style. In the other group the two adults led all six goslings, which somehow managed to follow precisely in line despite the rough waves.

By midday I was almost in Balerno and decided that after yesterday's long haul I'd stop there to re-charge the batteries and cure the pains in my chest/arms/throat. But there was nothing in Balerno and I didn't like the town anyway. It was crammed with school kids eating pies and chips all over the place. I passed the school and it was completely empty. Obviously the kids have to go out to get their own lunch, but to the detriment of the local population I think, who were nowhere to be seen (run for cover I expect) and surely to the detriment of the children's health. Not only the snacky unhealthy meals, but also the lack of games or activities such as you might have on the school premises. Just mooching about and eating in bored fashion. Anyway, that was Balerno at lunchtime. Which contrasted sharply with its outskirts, which were lovely. Coming down off the Pentland Hills there were fields of rape, little copses and sheep-farming right up to the edge of the town. And all this is only 10 miles from Edinburgh.

And so, on to Currie. I could have gone there in the first place from the Pentland Hills, except that I'd been so sure I'd find a B&B establishment in Balerno (because of its position, and the name itself which conjured up pictures of neat B&B establishments). Currie was a similar sort of place. On enquiring about B&Bs, I was directed to the Inn in the centre of town who did accommodation but were full up. They directed me to No.6 down the road but they were out, and there was no sign anyway so they'd probably given up. On I went. Reached the A71, no B&Bs. Reached Ratho, which hadn't looked very promising from the distance and was even less so from close up, but at least it was on my route. No B&Bs. The people at the Ferry Inn were very helpful and changed me lots of coins for the phone. They told me about Ratho Hall, but that was £50, Norton Hill House, about £85. Somebody thought there was a place in

Newbridge. Went there. Nothing in Newbridge. Went on through squally rainy weather and a bit weak at the knees by this time, thinking it would have to be Queensferry after all. Finally, in Kirkliston, where I'd been told earlier by someone who lived there, that there were no B&Bs, someone said: 'Och yes! There's one just down the rooooad there!' And so there was! Very nice, Heather and Dave. Heather was out, but Dave, after much reflection, did show me the room. In fact he showed me two rooms and wanted me to choose between soft beds here and harder beds there and all I wanted to do was to sink onto any bed at all! In his friendly fashion, he showed me all the maps and photos on the walls of his daughter's bedroom, and told me the stories of her travels that went with them. Warming to his theme he progressed into a detailed account of his own travels around Scotland. I was finding it increasingly difficult to stand up by this time, and when he eventually left me, I collapsed on to the bed and didn't move a muscle for at least half an hour! Later I measured about 18 miles on the map with the wheelie. And though I'd only had a bowl of soup in Ratho and was quite hungry, I couldn't face going out again. So I ate all the edible contents of my pack, dates, figs and nuts, and had most of the biscuits out of the tin in my room. Funnily enough I couldn't sleep for ages.

Tuesday 25 May
Kirkliston - Inverkeithing

Heather and Dave gave me the £3 change towards Leukaemia Research. Such a nice couple and so friendly, like all the Scots people I've met.

My voice had nearly disappeared this morning and a cold has started, but the sore throat is better and I'm feeling OK. Fixed bits of sheep's wool to my heels and set off.

Easy day thank goodness; only had to make it as far as North Queensferry, four or five miles away. Crossed the Firth of Forth road bridge, which was quite a thing. It took 25 minutes to cross and I had wonderful views of the rail bridge further up the firth. Took lots of pictures before and after, but on the bridge itself it was so windy I didn't care do anything except walk straight ahead, clutching firmly on to Stick! One of a group of construction men walking over the bridge asked to see my Stick and admired it greatly. When

I said it had come all the way from Land's End, he asked where I was going? We both laughed merrily as he said in the next breath, 'John O'Groats?' He clapped me on the shoulder and they all wished me luck and went on their way southwards, buffeted by the wind.

Jim would have liked the bridge. I never knew he was keen on bridges; it was Arianne who told me that.

At North Queensferry I decided not to stop after all because it was only midday, and walked on through a fine drizzle of rain to Inverkeithing, a rather dreary place. But I found a good B&B straightaway (£14) and this afternoon have done sterling work with the maps and pages from the Perthshire Tourist Information brochure I cut out weeks ago. I've telephoned to organise B&B for the next three nights, very satisfying.

I had a nice thought earlier as I was walking along the main road towards the Forth Bridge, that this is certainly where all the other 'End to Enders' have walked or ridden, Simcock[37], Ian Botham[38] and the rest. Not McCloy though of course, he'd have been clambering up some knoll or other he'd have managed to find somewhere between Edinburgh and the bridge!

Phoned Berwyn and he'd heard from the boys, all OK and no catastrophes with the bikes so far. Socky-locky[39] is now on insulin for his diabetes, so let's hope that will sort him out. Apparently he was covered in fleas when Berwyn got him to the vet's; his ears were lined with them!

Wednesday 26 May

Inverkeithing - Kinross

It's an amazing fact that I'm sitting here in Gairney Bank, Perthshire, watching the FOOTBALL! Manchester United are playing Bayern Munich in the European Final in Barcelona. Only about twice in my life have I ever watched an entire football match on television. Not even that, come to think of it - maybe it's a first! I'm relaxing in the hugely leathered upholstery of the guests' sitting

---

[37]. John Simcock. *End to End Stuff*, by John Simcock. Avon Books, 1996. John Simcock walked the 1086 miles of his route from John O'Groats to Land's End in two months.
[38]. Ian Botham walked from Land's End to John O'Groats in 1985, and repeated the walk in reverse direction in 1999. He walked the 850 miles (a main road route) in 34 days. Over the years, Ian Botham has raised more than £3.3 million for the Leukaemia Research Fund.
[39]. Socks, the cat, greatly loved by all the family.

room, very comfortable and I'm the only one here. There are other guests but they've all driven off into Kinross to eat. Kinross is about two miles away and I couldn't face the thought of a hike into town, even though I was quite hungry. Instead I've had a dainty supper of cheese portions, with dates to follow.

Today's walk was along a B road all the way, quite good but nothing special. I'd decided to ditch the original more off-the-beaten-track route for the sake of speed. The next two days will be better though, into the Ochil Hills, following McCloy's route in part. I got here quite early, mainly due to the rain that prevents loitering, and also because I hadn't realised the B&B is so far short of Kinross. But it's very nice and they're a friendly couple, a builder and his wife, who are also watching the football in their sitting room.

I'm going to have cheese omelette for breakfast!

The football is going into the second half now, Manchester United 1 - 0 down. Dan will be watching it in France and I bet he's in a state of complete silence by now. I'm glad he's got two other Man U supporters with him to share the agony!

Late addition: in the last five minutes Man U scored two goals and so are the European champions, as well as League and Cup Final winners.

Thursday 27 May
Kinross - Forgandenny

Even though I can't do all the wild mountainy stuff advocated by McCloy, I also know I'd be really pushed to do a straight main road journey. Those are the days I find most tiring, even when they're flat and/or not too busy. It's happened over and over again that when I'm in country lanes or on a long-distance path, with nothing but birds to hear and the countryside spread all around me, I feel immediately rejuvenated. The aches and pains disappear, I relax and all is right with the world. Today was one such day, and even though it was 16 miles and my legs came out in their habitual, 16-mile rash, I don't feel as knackered as I usually do after a day's road walk. It was beautiful, I didn't meet a soul, and the tiny lanes undulated up and down through the Ochil Hills, which at this end are not steep. The gorse was magnificent, I've never seen so much colour, and the air was full of its coconut smell mixed with May blossom. I spent ages watching a hare through the binoculars. There were a few farms dotted here and there on the lower slopes of the hills and the animals were all sporting offspring, calves, foals and lambs that are still quite small in these northern climes. Farms here are more industrial-looking, less picturesque than in England. As if they've taken up farming relatively recently, which perhaps they have.

There were larks, yellow-hammers, chaffinches in the lower parts, and lapwings, sea-birds and buzzards on the hills. This is only the second pair of buzzards I've seen since leaving the southwest of England, where they were so numerous. The ash trees are finally coming out and the oaks are now quite leafy. The hedgerows, mostly hawthorn, are full of pink and red campion, star of Bethlehem, cow parsley, blue bells, buttercups and the tender new shoots of unfurling bracken. The combined colours were superb. I made a mental note to include Broom and hawthorn in the new Jimmy garden.

I even heard a robin, the first for a while. And so I thought Jim-a-long is here too. I've been thinking that about robins for some weeks now. It's not so much the bird that reminds me of him (he was neither cute or cocky) as the song. So beautiful, and in that minor key. I think of Jim every time I hear it. It's getting a bit better I think; I haven't cried for a while, though funnily enough writing this, I begin to want to. I wonder how it will seem when I get home again.

The farmhouse B&B turned out to be a modern bungalow, but the farm is spread all around us and there are cows in the field directly outside my window. The very nice landlady said she'd do me some sandwiches, at 6.30 pm, she said. No sign yet but they're all outside having problems with the burglar alarm on the Landrover. I hope she hasn't forgotten because I'm quite hungry (ate all the food I'd bought in Kinross at lunchtime).

Booked Dunkeld, so that's all done now right up to the time Berwyn comes.

Friday 28 May
Forgandenny - Perth

Peed down with rain all day. The worst deluge was during the morning when I was making my sodden way along what should have been a lovely road by the banks of the River Tay. I started off in a fine drizzle, but quite soon it was teeming down and it never stopped, all the way to Perth. I was like a drowned rat by the time I reached the youth hostel (which I found with difficulty mainly because I couldna understand the directions in Scottish)! The warden took one look at me and lifted up the flap of his reception box to whisk me straight off to the drying room, 'Ye can change in there too!' he said. Even my Paramo trousers had given up and my legs were wet for the first time (but there was a reason for this: the straps dangling from my pack had been constantly drip-dripping onto the front of my trousers). It's just as well I was booked into the youth hostel because whatever else they may lack, they have excellent drying facilities. This one also has a washing machine and a dryer, so I'll be able to get all the chores done before I start off again on Sunday for the Big Push to the mountains!

Last night's landlady, May, was so nice (even though she had forgotten my ham sandwiches and I had to remind her in the end). She gave me £10 towards the LRF and refused to let me pay for the sandwiches. We stood in the hall for ages when I was saying goodbye. She told me all about her youngest daughter at University studying agriculture, and the girl's determination to get the experience she needs for cattle-farming. Despite being a star prize-winning student she had difficulty in getting a placement in the US farm of her choice merely because she's a girl. Lots of obstacles and successes, but the family so loving and supportive, combining modesty with their pride. All their children are in farming now; their son has a farm over the hill and the elder daughter married a farmer nearby. They rear a new breed of cattle - *black* Limousin.

When I left there it made me think a lot about families. As always, it comes back to Jim. If he'd had success earlier I feel he might be with us still. The last year of intensive work was good and I know how much he enjoyed it, and how happy he was with the new partnership, creating music on the computer. He loved all of that. But financially it was hard for him. When the band was signed to George Michael's outfit, the first thing he did was buy himself clothes and move into David's old flat. He wanted to live in more comfortable, salubrious surroundings.

He himself always maintained that he never had a hard time, emphatically denying any suggestion that the last winter had been hard, despite the long hours in the little studio, plus teaching guitar on at least two evenings a week and the weekend driving work. But he did admit that the weekend Argos lorry driving was irksome. He liked the driving part of it, but the employers treated the drivers badly, and exacerbated his constant struggle with money by arbitrarily changing methods of payment. He'd 'signed off' the previous summer, determined to be independent and get the social security people out of his hair. He'd had enough of the awful business of signing on, the endless forms and forever being made to feel guilty for claiming benefit in the first place. (He always reckoned he'd be paying it back in taxes when he finally made his millions).

If only he'd learnt, in his youth, to be more complaining, more stroppy. He was always so good-natured and sunny. He loved happy times and harmonious surroundings. So does everybody of course, but I think some people need it more than others. When he was upset, or even a bit unhappy, he became ill. It happened over and over again. I first noticed it in his playschool days, which he clearly didn't like much, though he never made any fuss about going there. A pattern developed whereby he'd go for a week or two, develop an ear infection or some other minor complaint. We'd go the doctor, get antibiotics, he'd get better, go back to school, and then the whole cycle would be repeated over again. In the end we gave up playschool altogether and he was absolutely fine, no more illness and as happy as a sandboy! What he really, really wanted was to go to Big School, proper primary school, where Michael went. But when he got there it wasn't so very different, though he was older of course and hardier.

It became apparent over the years that whenever things weren't quite right he'd spring a temperature or go down with flu-like symptoms. I remember the occasion when a man accosted him (verbally) as he was coming home from Wadhurst. Not surprisingly he was frightened, and by the time the policeman arrived to get all the details, Jim was in bed with a high temperature! When he was older, he'd collapse in an exhausted heap and just sleep for hours. It's ironic that the one who was physically the biggest and so strong looking was the most prone to illness.

I suppose what I think is that if he'd been able to vent his feelings more, he would have been healthier. He wasn't the easy-going fellow that people thought. Socially he was, he liked people and they liked him. But he was also serious and competitive. He was ambitious too, he wanted to do well and shine in his chosen field. It was perhaps hard for him to see all his friends doing well, and others buying houses, getting married. I think he felt pressured a bit. He wanted to be able to demonstrate that he'd 'made it'. And he did in the end. At least he had a tiny taste of the success he deserved so much. If only it had come sooner.

During the early spring of that year we knew he was getting tired and kept suggesting he take time off, but he wouldn't. Even after the 'single' was completed, he and James and Arianne felt they had to launch straight into writing the songs for the follow-up album. And knowing how caught up he was in that creative burst of energy I suppose we shouldn't have wanted it otherwise. Michael, David and Dan were so delighted with the (then) completely new intricacies of their music. It's one of the 'comforts' (I have a few) to know that Jim knew how impressed they were with it.

We could have given him some more money, but he hated accepting handouts all the time. He should have eaten a better diet, but I dare say he ate what he liked - beef, so cheap now because of BSE. He certainly shouldn't have smoked.

Maybe his getting leukaemia was nothing to do with any of these things. But in my own mind they are added risk factors. Added to the genes that I gave him, poor lamb.

8pm: The hostel here is good, a bit short on the old showers perhaps but otherwise it's got everything. I like being in a large youth hostel too, where there are lots of people milling about but you can be alone without embarrassment.

The wardens are most friendly and helpful. All of us more mature women have been put in the same dormitory, 12 of us tonight! In prime place by the window are some American visitors - mother and two daughters, searching for dead rellies in the cemetery.

Saturday 29 May
Day off; Perth

I hadn't intended having a day off in Perth, but as I was a day ahead of myself (after those long days when I couldn't get a B&B) it seems sensible and cheap to add on a night here. So today I've done all my washing, lots of eating and quite a bit of sightseeing. I visited the Art Gallery and Museum and went on a round-Perth bus trip that included Scone Palace, a beautiful building, the bit of it I glimpsed (didn't want to get off the bus, so lovely to just sit and be driven around). Got supplies of food in case there's not much on the road tomorrow. I'm getting edgy about the mountains. The YH warden, who is a bit of a character, a walker himself and usually full of jokes, says it's uphill from here on. Och aye. Also, that the wind in the Drumochter Pass is dreadful. He says I should eat pasta beforehand - anyone would think I was going to run the Marathon! All the same, I took to heart all that he told me because I could see he was being serious for once. I think he regards me as a bit of an odd ball.

I had a very nice lunch in a cafe next to the Museum, and thought about confidence. It's something I've acquired, if a bit late in the day! In the early days of the walk, I remember feeling quite conspicuous, and so obviously an outsider, togged up in walk gear and covered in backpack. It was impossible to walk around nonchalantly, appearing to know my way around, maybe even giving the impression that this was where I lived, as has been my wont in varying degrees throughout my entire life. So I had to conjure up a new persona for myself, which was roughly: *You may not know me and I might look odd, but I'm as good as any of you, and maybe it's me doing you the favour by gracing your funny little town with my presence!* That was way back in March (in Portreath, I think) and today I realized I no longer have to articulate the thoughts. In fact, I'm so far advanced in the confidence stakes, that I was thinking it could form the nub of an assertiveness course, all you'd have to do is dress the person up in outlandish clothes and send her or him out to a strange place for a while! If you absolutely cannot merge with your surroundings, there is no alternative to making the most of being different.

I've even got used to going into pubs on my own and I'm completely relaxed about eating in even quite smart places. I don't hang my head when the inevitable question, 'Just for one?' is asked with that hint of habitual disdain. I'm very happy to sit, eat and watch the others eaters, or not, as the case may be. They all have to talk to each other, fill up the silences, but I don't have to say a word. Very relaxing!

Sunday 30 May
Perth - Dunkeld
Here I am in Birnam, just south of Dunkeld, absolutely knackered. It was 17 miles minimum, probably more because of circling around the outskirts of Perth trying to get to the riverbank (there were massive road-works around the embankment in the town centre). And except for a couple of miles following the River Tay from Perth to Luncarty, it was hard road all the way. Had to stop lots of times because of 1) diuresis: three urgent pees in the space of three hours this morning, 2) foot trouble: bandage to left foot because of pain in the arch, and sheep's wool to sore little right toe, 3) sharp pains in left arm/shoulder/chest again. What a mess.

It was good weather though, sunny and not too hot. And the River Tay was glorious, so wide and majestic. Took lots of pictures.

Dunkeld, famous for being the scene of Macbeth, is also considered to be the Gate to the Highlands and there was certainly a feel of the mountains today. The hills around here are all clad in oak forest, Birnam Oak I suppose. Very lovely in their virginal fresh green.

Early to bed. Last night in the youth hostel, my second in the 'gels dorm', a vast American woman snored loudly all night long. It was awful. But there was entertainment as well, in the form of two Spanish girls who came in late and became convulsed with hysterical giggles when they heard the racket! They stuffed handkerchiefs into their mouths, almost suffocating with the effort of keeping quiet, but in the end gave up the struggle and first one, then the other, had to rush out into the corridor, where I could hear them exploding into absolute gales of laughter! Cheered me up no end. But the deafening racket roaring out of the bunk below got to them too, later on. Because of their late arrival they had to occupy the last two remaining bunks, one of which was next door to, and the other right above the snoring woman. And eventually the girls themselves made quite a noise too, one getting very cross, clicking her tongue and clapping her hands Spanish-style, all in vain, and the other trying to shush up her friend! The only person in the whole place who had a good nights sleep was the American woman herself. Poor thing perhaps, but we were fed up with. Goodness knows how she fitted in the lavatory; it was half her size.

Only two more days before I meet Berwyn again! It's four weeks since we were last together, the longest parting in our life. And tonight the boys and Tam and all the friends should be back from the bike ride in France.

Monday 31 May
Dunkeld - Pitlochry

Lovely day. Visited Dunkeld briefly in the morning and saw the cathedral (half of it roofless and ruined, the other half in use), and Thomas Telford's splendid bridge over the Tay. Dunkeld is an attractive place, quiet and gracious. Probably overrun with tourists later on in the day, but at 10am even on a Bank Holiday Monday, it was very good.

For the first four miles I walked alongside the Tay on a wooded, scenic path signed to Inver, which I just happened to see, and then on to the B road west of the Tay, also quiet and lovely. Now the Highlands were actually coming into view every now and then, with snow on their tops!

My big worry of the day was if the small bridge across the River Tay existed still, only a dotted line on the map. My landlord of last night said he was pretty sure it was still there, but I wondered why nobody else walks on this side of the river, so much nicer and with no traffic? I would have been really up the creek if the bridge hadn't been there, as it would have meant going on to cross the river at Aberfeldy, some seven miles further on, and completely out of the way. But there it was, what a relief! Privately owned and cross at your own risk, but as good and solid a bridge as you could wish for. From there, the last few miles were up a small lane that took off in Logierait, going through lovely wooded country and farmland all the way to Pitlochry.

Here, I found the youth hostel quite easily, too late to bag a bottom bunk, but it was only a six-bedded room and all very clean and spruce. In the same room were two very nice elderly Scotswomen on a walking holiday, sandals and ankle socks, snowy white hair, and as tough and spry as teenagers. 'We're well into our seventies!' one of them told me, as she leapt up into her top bunk. Interestingly, she later on confided to me that she always gets a rash on the lower part of her legs when she's walked a long distance. 'So do I!' I cried in delight!

Went down into the town for supper and sight-see, and gradually woke up to the fact that there were streams of vintage cars cruising slowly through the main street. It turned out there was going to be a parade in the recreation ground. I wasn't going to bother with it, but then heard the joyful strains of bagpipes in the distance, and found out that they would also be there! So I rushed back to the hostel for my camera and drifted down to the recreation ground with the rest of the population. For the next few hours we were treated (for the cost of £6) to Pipes, Highland dancing, Scottish dancing (there is a difference), accordion playing and the singing of Scottish songs. The sun was setting brilliantly on the surrounding hills and woods and it was quite a sight. A bit cold though and, despite the lovely bagpipes, I left after the first third of the programme, which didn't worry me too much because the second and third parts were going to be exact replicas of the first. There must have been at least 200 Morgan and MG cars, drawn up in a huge semi-circle for us to admire. They gleamed and shone in the setting sun and I thought how much Jim would have loved them, though I know he preferred modern sports cars.

I smile sometimes to think what his reaction would be if he knew one of the reasons for this walk is to compensate him for not being able to do things like this. The thought of even a short walk would be enough to put him off! But if he could have done it in a Ferrari now, or on a beautiful many-thousand cc Kawasaki motorbike - well, he'd certainly be up for that! And wouldn't it be a doddle, compared with his trip across the USA and back, on the ancient motorbike he bought over there that had some of its parts tied on with string. 'Guess how I got here?' he asked, when he rang us from Los Angeles. 'Motorbike!' and he couldn't keep the glee out of his voice! Then, knowing our dread of this form of transport, he kept quiet about returning to New York on the same bike, having spent the Greyhound bus-fare money we sent him, on a sleek, black leather jacket! Thinking about it now, I can't remember any other occasion when he openly went against our wishes. He wasn't a rebellious child, and as an adult I suppose it was typical of his character that he only told us afterwards, lest we should worry.

Tuesday 1 June
Pitlochry - Calvine

Lovely riverside walk most of the way to Killiekrankie, where there was a very good visitor centre. The River Garry ran deep along the bottom of a thickly wooded, steep-sided valley. So steep that some of the time you couldn't see the river at all. I went on a bit further to view the Soldier's Leap across the river from one rocky outcrop to another. He was fleeing the pursuing Jacobites and it must have been an incredible jump if true. Queen Victoria is said to have pronounced it 'impossible!' when she visited the site.

After that leafy interlude the road to Blair Atholl seemed long and hard, and after Blair Atholl even longer and harder. Had glimpses of the Castle though, gleaming white and turreted, most romantic-looking. And then on to Calvine, that most famous place in my memory! Calvine is the last outpost before the long stretch to Dalwhinnie, and if it weren't for this little place, the total distance with no place to stay would have been 22 miles. It was one of the few B&Bs I booked from home before I set off. I arrived about 3.30pm and Berwyn was there already! I'd not expected him to be there before evening. Lovely to see again the Companion of my Heart. New name.

Wednesday 2 June
Calvine - Loch Garry

We both set off together, me to walk the 12 miles to Loch Garry, where we arranged to meet, and Berwyn to do a bit of sightseeing at Blair Atholl. Loch Garry is just this side of the Drumochter Pass and so the worst bit is still to come. The first part was beautiful, mainly because of the birds. I walked along the tree-lined old A9, closed to traffic now, except for bicycles, and full of birches growing up out of the tarmac. The present A9 was close by, but not too intrusive. I think just about every bird that I'd heard on the journey was singing this morning, and it was glorious. I was listing them in my mind and I wish now I'd stopped to write them all down. There were all the garden birds, moorland birds and even some seabirds.

Only the last two or three miles were on the A9 proper, so it wasn't a bad walk at all. We met at Loch Garry at 2.30pm precisely, as arranged, and Berwyn was very pleased with Blair Castle, where there had even been a piper, piping tunes outside the front door. Then off to our B&B in Kingussie, which has fantastic views of the Cairngorms and the Inverness railway line from our bedroom window. A very friendly couple run the place, Berwyn thinks he's an ex-policeman but I think he's being unduly influenced by the display of handcuffs and old truncheons in the hall. My guess is that he's a printer; he's very thin and has a printer's face. Jenny, his wife, is large and jolly and laughs at everything. The place is very good and reasonable. They're terribly impressed with my walk and have told the story to all the other guests.

Thursday 3 June
Loch Garry - Crugenmore

The day of the Drumochter Pass! Berwyn dropped me off at Loch Garry again and as it was going to be another 12-mile day we arranged to meet at 2.30pm (4 hours at 3mph). Rained most of the way.

The Drumochter Pass is a bit grim and uninviting but on the whole not nearly as bad as I was expecting. Ever since the early days of planning the walk I'd been a bit worried about getting through the mountains, and felt even worse when I acquired the maps for that part and saw the great swirls of closely packed contour lines filling the page and just the one, direly straight, red road running through it. Most of the time (until I got to Perth) I'd imagined a parched, arid landscape, hot dry winds whirling through the Pass, and a dusty road snaking its way through the massive mountain range. A sort of cowboy scenario, with me dropping by the wayside for want of water (after all, I would be there in June)! Then, from Perth onwards, after my conversation with the YH warden who had advised me to wrap up well and eat pasta beforehand, I'd been picturing it as a massively gaunt place, cold, dark, snowy even, and me head down, battling against the wind howling and the rain sheeting through the Pass. Of course, the reality was neither of these extremes. It was darkish, rainy, and the mountains were neither so very high or so very dramatic. They were close-by though, and the clouds swirled low so that you couldn't see the tops, and the rain did indeed sweep down through the Pass. So I was glad to get to Dalwhinnie, where I stopped briefly to wring out my socks, sodden from walking through the wet grass verge.

Dalwhinnie, famous for its whisky distillery, is dismally unattractive. I didn't see anywhere to stay, so goodness knows where I would have slept had Berwyn not been here to ferry me to and fro. I passed quickly through it and was out onto General Wade's military road again, oyster-catchers and lapwings shouting the odds all the way. I found, dead by the side of the road, one of the little birds I've been trying to identify for the past few weeks. It's only about the size of a chaffinch or robin, with a yellow speckled breast. I've seen quite a lot of them and I wish I knew what it was.[40]

Met Berwyn at the appointed meeting place once more, exactly on time. He had been to the Highland Museum and other wonders and thoroughly enjoyed himself. In the evening we drove out to Aviemore and had a big meal in an Italian restaurant.

Friday 4 June

Crugenmore - Kingussie

Short day, only nine miles of uneventful, wet, road walking. Berwyn went on to Aviemore to pick up the photos and I spent the afternoon doing washing, and working out the journeys for the last stage. I also managed to ring up and book quite a lot of B&Bs in places where I thought they would be scarce. Felt very pleased with myself for doing that.

We had a secret meal of bread and cheese and wine and cake in our bedroom. I always feel a bit guilty about doing that, though there's no reason why we shouldn't. Some B&Bs have notices in the bedroom though; I remember one banning the eating of all Cooked Food in the room.

---

40. Tom Isaacs, my friend and fellow 'End to Ender' who kindly read the manuscript for me, begs me never to try and find out what this little bird actually is. And so I haven't.

End of Stage IV! We added up all the mileage and as I thought, this stage was big in terms of distance - 237 miles, and only one day off. The next stage will be about 40 miles less I think.

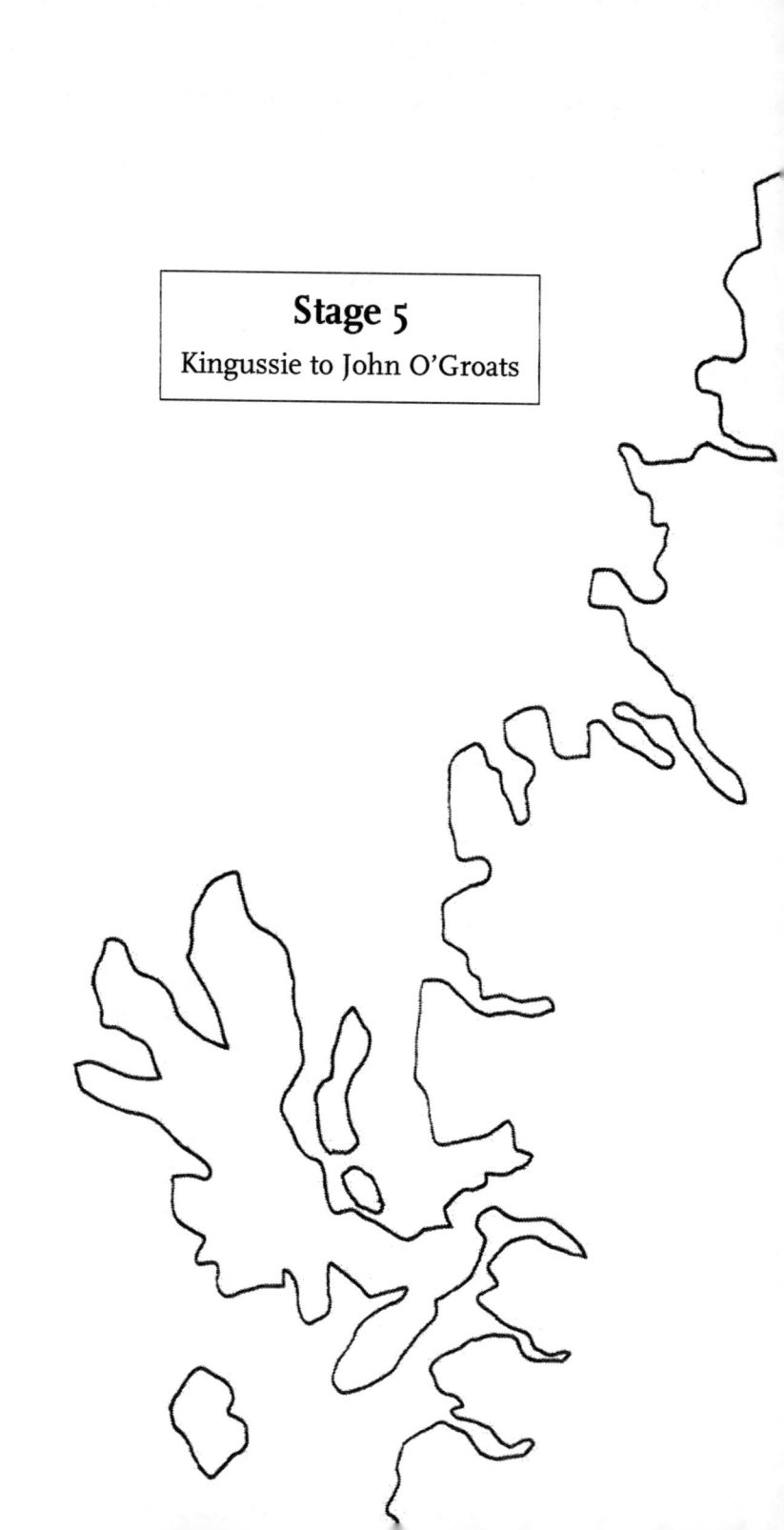

Stage 5
Kingussie to John O'Groats

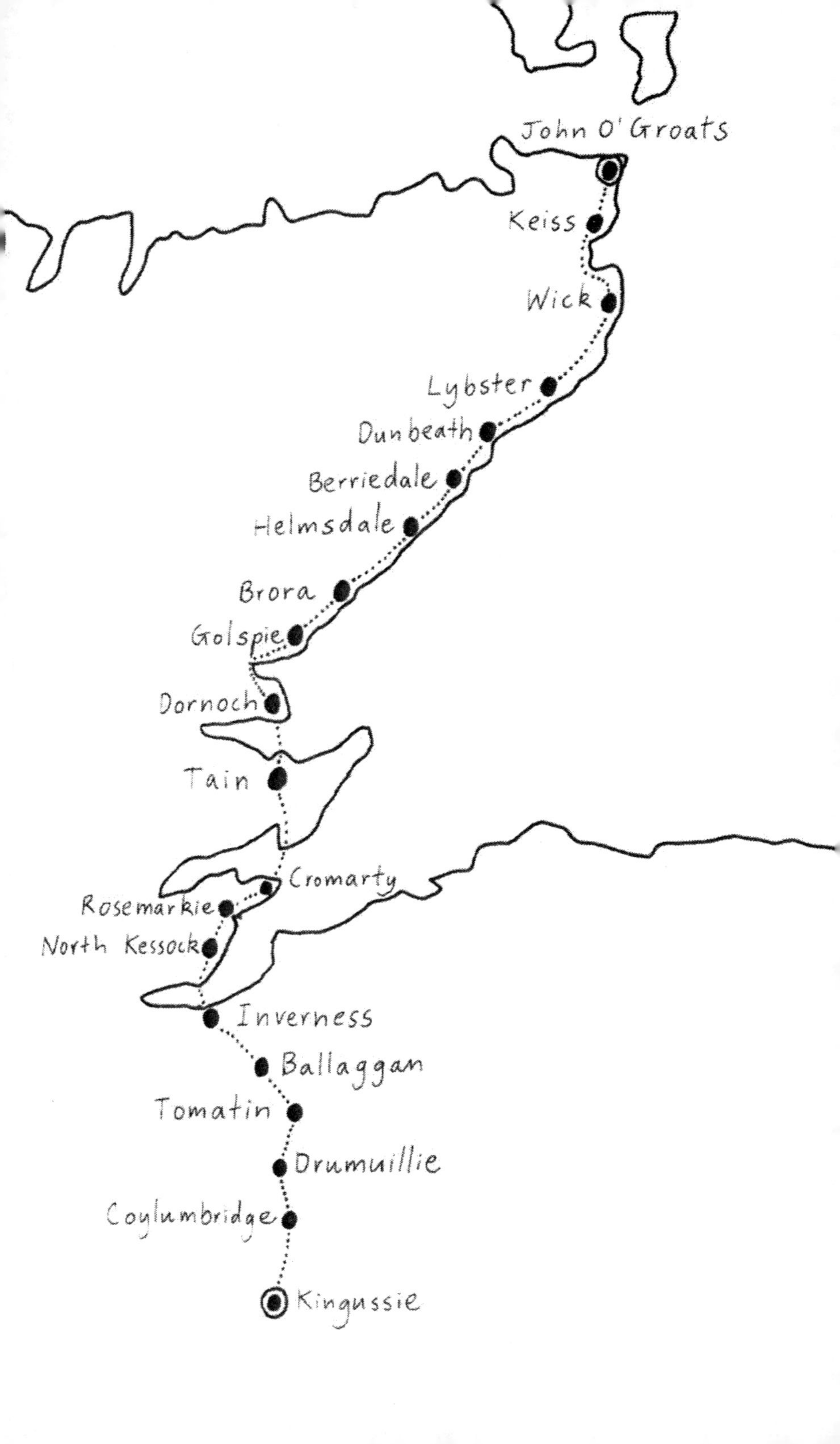
John O'Groats
Keiss
Wick
Lybster
Dunbeath
Berriedale
Helmsdale
Brora
Golspie
Dornoch
Tain
Cromarty
Rosemarkie
North Kessock
Inverness
Ballaggan
Tomatin
Drumuillie
Coylumbridge
Kingussie

Kingussie to John O'Groats

Cairngorms - Culloden - Inverness - Black Isle - John O'Groats
Saturday, 5 June - Saturday 26 June

OS 35 Kingussie + OS 36 Grantown

Kingussie, Kincraig, Feshiebridge, Inverdruie, **Coylumbridge**.   13 miles

Coylumbridge, Pityoulish, Boat of Garten, **Drumuillie**.   7 miles

OS 36 + OS 36 Kingussie

Drumuillie, Kinveachy Lodge, General Wade's Military Rd., Sluggan, Inverlaidnan Hill, Slochd, **Tomatin**.   16 miles

OS 35 + OS 27 Nairn & Forres

Tomatin, Loch Moy, Auchnahillin, Craggiemore, **Ballaggan**.   11 miles

OS 27 + OS 26 Inverness

Ballaggan, Clava Lodge, Culloden, Westhill, **Inverness**.   8 miles

Inverness, Kessock Bridge, **North Kessock**.   3 miles

OS 26 + OS 27

North Kessock, Drumsmittal, Munlochy, Corrachie, Avoch, Fortrose, **Rosemarkie**.   12 miles

OS 27 + OS 21 Dornach

Rosemarkie, Raddery, Poyntzfield, Udale Bay, Jemimaville, **Cromarty**.	13 miles
Cromarty, Nigg Ferry, Balnabruaich, Arabella, **Tain**.	11 miles
Tain, Morangie, Dornoch Firth Bridge, Cuthill Sands, Lonemore, **Dornoch**.	9 miles
Dornoch, Fourpenny, Loch Fleet, The Mound, Balblair Wood, **Golspie**.	12 miles

OS 17 Helmsdale

Golspie, Brora.	6 miles
Brora, Helmsdale.	10 miles
Helmsdale, Ord of Caithness, Baobae Monument, **Berriedale**.	9 miles
Berriedale, Dunbeath.	6 miles

OS 11 Thurso & Dunbeath

Dunbeath, Latheron, **Lybster**.	8 miles

OS 11 + OS 12 Thurso & Wick

Lybster, Bruan, **Wick**.	15 miles
Wick, Keiss.	8 miles
Keiss, John O'Groats.	9 miles
Total	**186 miles**

(19 days walking, average 9.8 miles per day. Days off: 3)

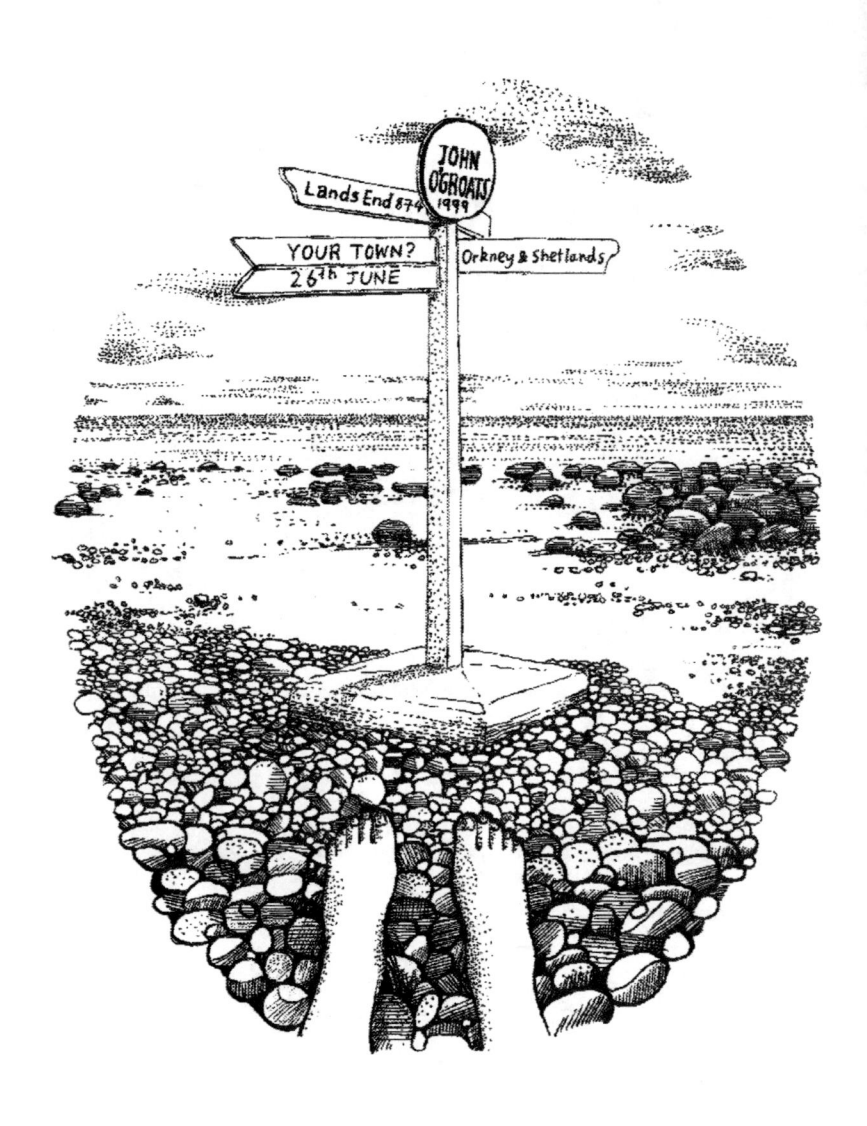

End of the road.

Stage V

Saturday 5 June
Day off; Kingussie

We left our B&B amid fond farewells and drove to the Cairngorms and Lake Morlich. The latter was a bit disappointing, all canoes and caravans. But the chair lift to the Cairngorms was open and we went up the two stations to the top of the mountain. Initially it was a bit bleak up there, but on walking further up to the summit, a whole new vista opened up to the south. It was magnificent; mountain peaks as far as the eye could see against a dramatic backdrop of wondrously piled-up storm clouds. We were lucky to see it because by the afternoon it was raining hard, and the chair lifts were closed.

Booked in to a B&B at Coylumbridge, one night for Berwyn and two for me. We drove towards Loch Eileen where we'd hoped to have a picnic supper, but by the time we got there it was sleeting hard and freezing, so we ate our picnic in the car and came back for an early night.

Sunday 6 June
Kingussie - Coylumbridge

Berwyn dropped me off in Kingussie at about 10 o'clock this morning. The miserable business of saying goodbye was made worse by the miserable weather - freezing wind and rain. I walked through the deluge along the B road as far as Kincraig, where I crossed the River Spey and took the footpath towards Feshiebridge. From there I followed the little road south of the Spey all the way to Inverdruie, next to Coylumbridge. It would have been a lovely walk had the rain stopped even slightly.

I feel extraordinarily tired, though it hasn't been a long day. I hate it when Berwyn goes, even though this is the last time. I'm absolutely terrified that something will happen to prevent this whole thing ending OK so that we can get back to our normal life. I could hardly bear the 'next time I see you it will be the end of the journey' sort of remark, lest we should be tempting fate and some catastrophe will intervene between now and then. Silly and illogical, but I can't quite banish the thoughts from my mind.

I'm going to finish my book, Henry James's *What Maisie Knew*, long in the reading, mainly because of its convoluted sentences. Good though, despite its difficulties.

Monday 7 June
Coylumbridge - Drumuillie

Here I am in a lovely clean room with views across field, moor and distant woods. The B&B garden is unfenced and merges with the view. For the last half-hour I've been watching a curlew and its chick. Chick is padding about in the rough grass in the garden whilst mother circles around in the air, calling every now and then, and landing occasionally to check on chick.

How much nicer here than the B&B of the last two nights, which was a bit stinky - and the elderly landlady was intrusive. She was always hanging about, and this morning had cleared the sheets off my bed during the few minutes I was out of the room having a wash, and was back in there again during the time I was having breakfast, making up the bed! It was an unofficial B&B though; she was the friend of a B&B establishment that was full up. And it was only £14. But where I am now is the same price and the contrast is amazing. I got here, wet and cold, about 3pm, and it's a real haven. The youngish couple whose place it is are both very nice and the room is sparklingly clean with TV, tea-making facilities, all the things you need (and were absent in the last place). Spotless bath and I had a big soak. Because there's a pile of Readers Digests as well as the TV, I haven't missed not having a book.

Today's walk was good, if a bit wet. The small road from Coylumbridge went through some lovely country and I saw as well as heard a cuckoo. Loch Pityouish was beautiful and I could just see the peak of the Cairngorms in the distance, snow-capped from yesterday's weather. There was no traffic at all. I had lunch in a large, empty hotel in The Boat of Garten, run, but not owned, by a couple who had fled the increasing violence in South Africa. They had gauged the risks to be unacceptable when their second baby was born and are now trying to acclimatise themselves to a substantially different life in this chilly, remote, but ultra-safe outpost of the UK! They were a really nice couple. The husband blamed the present troubles on South Africa's lost generation of children, uneducated because of the school boycotts throughout the 70s and 80s, and now grown into their twenties, still seemingly without prospects.

I had originally intended going on to the RSPB place near the Boat of Garten to see the ospreys, but it was an extra two miles out of the way and I didn't have the energy.

Berwyn got back in *one day!* I phoned just now and he said he'd not bothered to stop anywhere last night and had arrived home about 8.30pm. All well.

Later: I've just checked out of the window because I heard the curlew calling again, and chick is still there, plus there's a deer in the garden now as well. It's grazing and scratching itself, quite relaxed. There's a main road (the A95) the other side of the house, so I'm pleased my window looks this way.

Tuesday 8 June
Drumuillie - Tomatin

Most of the way on General Wade's Military Road, which at this point is no more than a grassy track. But all went according to plan, following McCloy's instructions and except for two places I didn't get badly lost. Downpours and cloudbursts of rain all day long. I saw several isolated deer and then, later on, a herd of a hundred or more, so it may have been a farm. They were very wild and shy, much more so than in Wadhurst Park.

If the day had been drier it would have been a stupendous walk, very varied, going through forest, rough moor and farmland. At one point the track went through a wide shallow river, which I tried to forge by leaping from stone to stone but ended up wading through. Later on, much worse, I had to cross a perilously high arched bridge that was almost a ruin, with no sides or supports or anything! Just grassy remains on the stone foundation, must be one of General Wade's. I dithered for quite a while, sizing up my chances of survival if I was to remove my footwear and wade through the river instead, but it was fast flowing and looked quite deep, so in the end I had to cross the bridge, hoping for the best!

The last stretch, from the point where General Wade's road (path) joined up with the A9, along the road to Tomatin, was neverending. This included a long haul up to the top of Slochd Mor pass, and it felt very exposed indeed in the mist and driving rain. Worse than Drumochter Pass in some ways. I think the whole day was about 16 miles, probably quite a bit more because of getting lost at one point, and I didn't stop at all because of the rain (except for the minutes spent gathering courage to cross the dreadful bridge, and other minutes trying to work out where exactly I was on the map). So I felt completely knackered on arrival.

The B&B arrangement, set up in Kingussie Tourist Information Centre, had been that the landlady would get me fixed up in the village somewhere, she herself being fully booked. I have it down in my notebook: 'Tomatin - somebody in village will have me,' and it was a nice comforting thought, conjuring up a picture of a close-knit community where everyone looks after everyone else, including stray visitors to the village. This impression was confirmed when I got here and a small boy on a bicycle escorted me down the main street to the door of the house. However, it was all a ruse, as Colin would say! She wasn't full up, but objected to paying the 10% TIC booking charge! And as I'd have had to pay my £1.50 to them as well, as she says, this way she gets the people and we all pay less! In fact, on hearing that the walk was connected to a charity she did what she usually does for walkers, and gave me her own guest-room for £10.

Had a big steak at the Tomatin Inn and was in bed and unconscious by 8.15pm. (I'm writing all this the next day).

Wednesday 9 June
Tomatin - Ballagan Farm

I'm in this remote farmhouse where the mobile phone won't work and there's not a kiosk for miles, so I got through to Berwyn on the house phone. I'm in a minuscule room, the smallest, bar one, of the entire trip. And it's a bit cold, no central heating. I've got Liz's windcheater on over my nightie.

The day was good, bright and sunny, and after a couple of miles along the A9 out of Tomatin I was on a B road. No traffic at all and after a long foresty bit, the road ran into the most lovely, peaceful stretch of open moorland, with a fast-flowing river running through the middle. The only sounds were the river and a positive cacophony of curlews, lapwings and oyster-catchers. I think I disturbed the curlews because they were particularly vociferous. Despite their protests, I stopped there for quite a while. It was too good to miss and I lay in the heather in the warm sunshine eating the remains of food from my rucksack. Later I turned off onto an even smaller road to get to my farmhouse B&B, which is close to Culloden Moor and the sites of various Pictish remains (see them tomorrow). This is a really beautiful area and so remote, you wouldn't think it's only a few miles from Inverness.

Haven't been feeling very good since I got here though, probably after yesterday's long haul. Got here quite early and the thoroughly welcoming landlady gave me tea and home-made cakes. I felt so tired I went to sleep for a bit and then woke up feeling terribly sad. My mind goes over the same old things, why did Jim get ill, where is he now? I know by now there are no answers. How I wish I'd given him more money, or bought him shoes or boots. He loved boots. I just wish I could have him here again. I wish he'd had the chance to wear the summer sandals he bought for Thailand - if he could at least have had the holiday.

Thursday 10 June
Balaggan Farm - Inverness

Got off to a good start and first of all saw the Clave burial chambers, dating from two or three thousand years BC. There were six or seven of them, in two groups, very well preserved. Then I called in at the Visitor Centre at Culloden Field, which was most interesting, and I've now come to grips with the whole Jacobite, Bonnie Prince Charlie saga. So much history has been a blur to me in the past, and it's very satisfying to get at least bits of it straight in my mind, and to be able to link up that era of history with later eras, such as the clearances, General Wade and the rest.

I spent an hour or two in the Visitor Centre before going on to Inverness. It was an easy day, only eight miles. Found the youth hostel in its new venue, huge and quite modern. I was glad to see the laundry room, and had a quick shower so I could wash all my clothes before going into town. Bought Dan's birthday present (tartan shirt) and generally did bits and pieces. Sent off maps and old books to Berwyn. Had tea, had supper. Heard the sound of pipes and rushed to the spot: it was a lone piper accompanying a troupe of 14 little girls and one boy who were giving a display of Scottish dancing in the precinct. I tried to visit the castle but it was closed, though there was a good statue of my friend Flora Macdonald up there. Inverness is a bit of a hotch-potch of old and really ugly concrete new, all wodged together so it's impossible to appreciate either. I heard it's the fastest growing city in Europe, and it looks like it too, massive new building and construction sights everywhere.

Tomorrow I've only got to get myself to North Kessock, just across the bridge, a grand total of two miles! I hope to see dolphins and whales and have another half day off. I've got two further days off to take later on as well, in order to spin out the time before getting to John O'Groats. I've worked out I could easily be there by Wednesday 23rd June. Still, it will be good to be slower and more relaxed, and to savour the last two weeks, because I'll certainly never have a time like this again.

Friday 11 June
Inverness - North Kessock

Probably about three miles in the end. Crossed the bridge over the Moray Firth from where there should have been superb views, had the weather been better. I could see snow on the mountains towards the northwest though.

I'm not feeling very good, got a tummy upset, but that's not the real problem. I've felt on the brink of tears all day. It started as I was walking along the main road to get to the bridge, and I was glad of the isolation that walking in an unknown town gives you. I don't know why it is, how suddenly I find myself almost drowning in memories of certain days, or particular incidents that occurred during those long hospital weeks, memories that were unbearable in the early days after he died, and are now as bad as ever when they crop up, seemingly out of nowhere.

After the bridge there was a distance of only a few yards to get to North Kessock, down some steep steps to the village on the shore. There I was greeted by a sudden waft of sea air, mixed with seaweed

- one of my favourite smells. I stood in the still air on the edge of the Firth and had one of those moments that I felt I'd always remember. But the nostalgia associated with the smell of the sea made me mournful all over again, and in the end I had a good howl in the privacy of my B&B room.

Later on I had a big platter of fish and chips in the little café down in the village and that has cured my queasy tummy!

Saturday 12 June
North Kessock - Rosemarkie

Still feeling a bit down, but the walk was mostly good despite the fine drizzle of rain that continued on and off all day. Started off with a country lane going up through Drumsmittal into small hills and an increasingly agricultural landscape. Lots of Highland cattle, and I passed a field of llamas too. Then on to Munlochy, which was pretty enough except that all the grey stone buildings made it look a bit dreary in the rain. Looked rather as it sounds in fact. Further on was the Munlochy Bay bird sanctuary. Haven to large numbers of winter visitors, the notice said. Waterfowl, teal, curlews, greylag goose, shelduck, oyster-catchers. Shooting was 'limited and restricted' during this time! Some haven, I thought.

Avoch (pronounced Och) was a lovely little place and I was tempted to take one of the dolphin-sighting boat trips. Seeing dolphins on this part of the Moray Firth is more or less guaranteed normally, but this year the numbers have plummeted and there is increasing concern regarding their welfare. Some say the sheer number of motorboats taking tourists out to view the dolphins is probably contributing to their demise (if they have demised, maybe they've just pushed off to quieter waters). I was tempted, but in the end decided to press on, as I'd no B&B booked.

Arrived in Fortrose where I'd been told there would be plenty of B&Bs but didn't see a single one, so, after a yummy prawn cocktail in a teashop, I walked on to Rosemarkie. Still no B&Bs. In the end the landlady of a pub down on the seashore said she knew of one and rang up to book me in, whilst I chatted with her two fixtures, one old, one young ('I'm Ian ... pleashed to meet you' ...) I'd passed the B&B already, about a mile back up on the main road, but they didn't have the sign up. It was a lovely house set in a big leafy garden overlooking the firth. Next morning I was told that the house, only 80 years old, was built by a local man who'd made his fortune as a timber merchant in London. He returned, built the house, with its garden running all the way down to the sea and then became a recluse. He never ever went out again and his only activity was shooting rabbits out of his bedroom window.

Sunday 13 June
Rosemarkie - Cromarty

Feel better today. It was a good walk and for once it wasn't raining. I went across the Black Isle from east to west along quiet lanes, through well kept rich-looking farmland - the land that is, not the farms, which seemed poor with collapsing sheds and run-down bungalow farmhouses. The living is obviously hard. But I've been told that the soil is very fertile and it's called the Black Isle because of the dark rich soil. For me, it was only spoilt by forest and I wondered why, if the soil was so good, they had to cover huge stretches with conifer plantations? Despite that, the road was lovely, and magical in places as I got nearer to the Cromarty Firth. The tops of oil rigs were poking out of the landscape in the distance. Oil rigs marooned in a wave-less sea. Getting closer, I glimpsed the firth now and then too, and then there it all was: sea, oil rigs, cloud-capped hills beyond, making a really splendid sight. I felt so pleased I'd come this way.

The last bit of today's journey was a longish stretch up the tranquil western coast of the Black Isle, all along Cromarty Firth to the town of Cromarty at its tip. There are dolphins in the firth here as well apparently, but I didn't see any. Didn't see any red kites either, which the area is famous for. Nor ospreys, but there had been one sighted from the RSPB hide that I went into at Udale Bay at 11.30am that day! I was there at 1.20pm and only saw a couple of swans.

Cromarty is the nicest place I've been in for ages. Rosemarkie was pretty, but this is a gem of a place. I went on an exploration around the town, its narrow streets lined with Georgian houses. The Courthouse is the famous attraction, having won awards for its innovative tourist demonstration of court proceedings, jail cells etc. Closed to me because it's Sunday. The sky was superb and I watched the sun going down as I ate my supper in the porch of the

Royal Hotel. I had to keep rushing out to take another photo, it was so good: shocks of dark dramatic cloud, edged with gold from the setting sun and all reflected in the calm, still sea. Impossible to connect those three shining oil rigs, resplendent in a glory of red and gold, with anything as mundane as oil.

It's 7.30pm and I'm waiting for Corrers. I've got a TV in my room for the first time for about a week. It's Sunday and it's 7.30pm but all there is on ITV is Grand Prix racing. Alright for Jim. I wouldn't mind, except that I don't know whether Corrers was on earlier and therefore I've missed it, or whether it will follow the Grand Prix. It's lap 67 now.

This is a very expensive B&B (four stars) so I didn't want to stop out too long, must make the most of it! I'm going to make hot chocolate now and I've already eaten all the sweets and most of the biscuits. I have a splendid bathroom down the corridor, exclusive to me. The landlady is a bit like Mrs.Bouquet in *Keeping up Appearances*.

Ferry tomorrow, Cromarty to Nigg. I'm very glad I went back to Plan A and came via Cromarty and the Black Isle. It had been my original choice; indeed Cromarty was one of the 'must-see' places, mainly because of the shipping forecast. Cromarty, Dogger, Finisterre, Malin Head ... you listen and wonder what it's like out there, in those far away, sea-swept places. For a while I'd changed my mind about coming this way, partly because nobody else seemed to and partly because it involves the use of a ferry. McCloy is very strict on not using ferries - or even the little train that crosses Morecambe Sands. 'Would you be able to tell your grandchildren you walked all the way to John O'Groats if you did?' he asks. After mulling it over awhile, I thought, 'Yes! I'd have no probs. with that.' I'll have walked every inch of the way, except across estuaries and strips of sea. And for me, the route was always more important anyway than any ideological nicety. I would have missed the southern end of the Lake District for example, if I hadn't crossed Morecombe Sands in the little train (traipsing all the way up the estuary and then down again was always a non-starter)! With regard to Cromarty, after due consideration I reverted to the original plan because the Black Isle looked so inviting on the map, and also because I met someone who comes from there and said it was beautiful. The final incentive was of course the ferry itself! Love ferries.

Forgot to mention that a couple of days ago I saw a yellowhammer. I hear them practically every day, like at home, but hadn't seen one until then. The moment it realised it had landed in sight of me, Great Scott! it was off again. Also today, I saw an oyster-catcher chick, on the shores of Cromarty firth, and ironically, the only reason I saw it was because of the racket its parents were making a short distance away, desperate to distract my attention away from it.

Monday 14 June
Cromarty - Tain

Well, here I am in a little house on the High Street of Tain, which I have all to myself and free of charge! I hadn't pre-booked for Tain because it's a sizeable place and I hadn't thought it would be necessary. But when I arrived and enquired at the Tourist Information Centre it turned out there wasn't a bed to be had in the whole of Tain. This was because of a sudden influx of engineers from the oil refinery at Nigg. Apparently they periodically flood into town during their stints at the oil works and when that happens all the B&Bs in Tain fill up and there's no place for tourists. This makes quite a lot of people unhappy, tourists for one; also the TIC, and also the B&B landladies because they can never organise a nice regular income. But the TIC person was very helpful and rang a friend who had a house that she didn't use, and having been described over the phone as a 'nice lady' I was sent down to the shop and told to ask for Morag. And here I am! Moreover, when she heard what I was doing and that it was for the LRF Morag insisted I stay here free of charge, and just give a donation to the fund. The Scots are terrifically hospitable and generous. Morag was a widow who had remarried but retained this, her old house. She no longer lets it because of the damage done by previous people - £200 worth of cigarette burns all over the dining room table.

So, I had a good walk after the short but happy ferry crossing (I was the only passenger) and despite a stretch along the A9, it hasn't been a bad day at all. The rain kept off most of the time and Tain is an attractive small town with historic, royal and religious connections. I visited the local museum and learnt that St Dunstell was born here in 1000. He became a saint and his relics were carried here from Ireland. On his account, King James IV (or V) of Scotland used to make an annual pilgrimage here, but unfortunately was killed shortly after the last one. Which just goes to show.

Had a long chat with Berwyn who'd been worried because I'd seemed unhappy a couple of days ago. I don't know why I felt so miserable then, unless it's because the end is in sight and with it the realisation that this phase is nearly over and it will be back to reality again quite soon. Or more precisely, back to the pretence of reality. I think that is what has been a bit of a strain in the past: the continual pretence that everything is OK, alright, getting back to normal, 'acceptance'. All the futile phrases that mean 'get on with your life now'. Not that any of our family and friends have ever suggested anything like that. They are superb, sensitive to everything and falling over themselves being supportive. The fault is in me. I can't weep before them and I can't change that. It's become habit now. In the early days I really felt that if I didn't keep a tight grip on myself I'd literally go mad. Gradually those feelings receded, I know I won't 'lose it' now, but I'm still stuck with only wanting to think, feel and howl in private.

Tuesday 15 June
Tain - Dornoch

I haven't mentioned the money or the press interview! Morag rang me in her house last night, to see if I was alright and to tell me that her American husband was completely bowled over by what I was doing and wanted to contribute to the cause. She also wanted to know whether the press were involved and thought very emphatically that they should be informed. Leave it to me, she said! So, when I returned to the shop this morning a reporter was waiting to interview me there and then, and Morag will send me a copy of the article when it's printed in the Ross-shire Something. Fame at last! She also gave me a £50 note for the LRF from her husband, far and away the biggest donation I've received. I shall remember Tain for its friendly hospitality as well as being an historic and attractive place.

Fine sunny day and I saw lots of seals. First, from the bridge going over Dornoch Firth and later when I was having a picnic lunch on the northern shores of the firth. Also, the RAF was breaking the sound barrier every few minutes as they flew out across the coastline. CRASH!

Dornoch is a 'pleasant town' as McCloy puts it, but I felt I'd seen most of what there was to see by the evening. I made a whistle stop tour of the 13th century cathedral, that is, I looked in through the front door, and I walked a considerable distance across the sands dunes via the famous golf course. So although I'd originally intended to have a day off here, I changed my mind and decided to go on to Golspie tomorrow instead.

This evening I had a jolly time in the bar of the hotel over the road from my B&B. I made the acquaintance of a nice Australian man and also collected £40 for LRF! This was a cheque (£20) from a woman and her husband on holiday, whose four year-old grandchild had died of leukaemia. They'd overheard our conversation and as they were leaving came over to me and gave me the cheque. She was really sweet and said, 'Until you go through it yourself, you can never know what it's like.' After they'd gone my Australian friend said, with tears in his eyes, that he also wanted to donate something, and he gave me a £20 note. Despite this, I had a merry evening. He was such a nice fellow and it was good to have conversation while eating for once.

Wednesday 16 June
Dornoch - Golspie

I was glad I'd decided not to have a day off in Dornoch because it rained on and off throughout the day. Even so I had a great walk, one of the best. From Dornoch to Loch Fleet Nature Reserve was along a quiet lane with glimpses of the sea. My usual birds returned to accompany me, curlews and oyster-catchers. They hate me and make a dreadful to-do, but I love them. Then, at the nature reserve, there were literally hundreds of birds: gulls, oyster-catchers, mallards, herons (actually saw one catching a fish several times) a whole flock of eider, and further away on a sandbank airing their wings, cormorants. The loch was beautiful - not spectacular, just quietly peaceful, gorgeous cloudy skies contrasting with the muted colours of the loch. Took lots of pictures and dallied there for quite a while. Then, after a dreary mile of A9 in the teeming rain, I turned off into a track leading to the northern edge of the loch. The track, marked on the map, eventually led onto Golspie golf course and by then the rain had stopped but it was blowing a gale instead. I was nearly whisked off my feet a couple of times and so was Stick. The sky was a glorious mass of navy blue clouds chasing each other over the duney golf course. It was quite dramatic.

Got to my B&B in the main street and immediately decided that yes, I would stay for a second night and have my day off here in Golspie. The B&B is OK and the sea is just the other side of the garden (the 'prom', as my retired English landlady calls it, is a concrete path running along the shore, and each of the terraced houses has a back gate leading onto it).

Thursday 17 June
Day off; Golspie

Morning: I'm sitting on this quiet beach about a mile out of Golspie and thinking what luck I kept my day off for today. Dunrobin Castle sits massively behind me, only a stone's throw away and I might visit it later on, but right now all I want to do is stay here, beside the seaside, beside the sea! Especially as the sun has now come out and it's quite warm. Three cormorants on a rock near the water's edge are spreading their huge flappy wings to the sun, and so I've taken a leaf out of their book and am now down to bare feet, rolled-up trousers and short-sleeved shirt. As warm as that!

I can see the A9 running north along the coast up to my left. Tomorrow I will be able to walk all the way along the beach though, or if the tide is up, along a track at the top of the beach, as far as Brora. Unfortunately I've no map of this area, the one section I'd failed to get photocopied. I feel a bit lost without a map now; it's become second nature to scrutinise the day's route, and I check it out all the time when I'm walking. It's especially necessary in Scotland where I feel less confident about going just anywhere, for example, a short cut through fields. Although in theory you've the 'right to roam,' in practice you never see anybody else doing that, and judging by the startled reaction of sheep and the lively interest of cows and bullocks (to say nothing of the frequent sightings of bulls) not many people do. So I tend to be very law-abiding and non-intrepid and only go along a footpath if it's clearly marked on the map. After Brora the A9 is the *only* road, so it may be hard going at times, especially where it starts to climb steeply. The cliffs are high and you can't get down to the sea. Still, will I care? So close to the end, I shouldn't think so!

There's a heron down there now, but it doesn't look as rich a fishing ground as Loch Fleet yesterday. Earlier there was one of those little dippy birds - black and white, walking very fast in all directions, catching sand-flies? Is it a Sand-piper? Or a dipper? There are so many birds I have to look up when I get home.

I've now been here about three hours and the only other living things I've seen are the cormorants, oyster-catchers and the wee dippy birds. This is certainly one of my best days. Probably one of the days I'll look back on when I'm home again, as 'real life' gathers momentum and I become encapsulated by people and events. A mental resolution has been taking shape over the last few weeks: not to let life get too busy. By most standards my life is pretty unfettered anyway, but I think it needs to be even more so, and it could easily be, if I only let it. I shall stop saying, 'Oh! I've got so much to do, Oh! I'm so busy!' and just *do less* and *be less* busy, not waste time and mental energy talking about it.

The tide is coming in and now there are seven cormorants on a more distant rock, their previous one under water. Like life, you have to find a new rock on which to stand. Facile observation perhaps, but true. I do know our family rock is still there, even if it is submerged in its original form.

1.45 pm: There are now 14 cormorants on the rock, collected there after all the other airing places have gradually become submerged, and the tide is coming in quite fast now. I saw a great blackbacked gull catch what I though was a big fish and fly with it to the shoreline, where it dropped it and made several stabs at eating it. Then the gull's mate came along and they both necked for a bit before flying off, leaving the catch behind. Perhaps it wasn't edible after all.

I've seen so much death on this trip. Fish-eating gulls and herons, sheep herded into trucks headed for the abattoir (yesterday by Loch Fleet was the last lot), dead lambs in the Wye valley, all the creatures dead by the side of the road that I've listed in my notebook. The screeching and crying of oyster-catchers and curlews at my approach, warding off the threat of death to their offspring. All the graveyards I've passed, all the cemeteries - hundreds of thousands of corpses and graves lining the country. Death is so much a part of life that we're scarcely aware of it most of the time. Until something happens to make you aware that actually death is the reality, and all the rest is mostly inconsequential.

Evening: When I finally dragged myself away from the beach idyll I felt I ought to go and at least look at Dunrobin Castle since it was so close. McCloy said the grounds were free and I didn't pay anything, though I found out later I should have done. I moseyed around the formal gardens for a bit and then found I'd timed it perfectly to see a demonstration by the falconer. He first of all showed us a HUGE Egyptian owl, then a peregrine falcon and lastly a buzzard. All did their flying tricks, getting bits of chicken and rabbit in return, very impressive. I was especially pleased to see the buzzard at close quarters, the bird that has accompanied me for so much of the way. What a perfect day off!

Friday 18 June
Golspie - Brora

Lovely walk, the best for ages. The weather wasn't sunny like yesterday, but warm and windy and threatening rain so there were beautiful clouds. I walked all the way along the shore, a track that led past Dunrobin Castle and yesterday's playtime, past a 2000 year-old broch perched high up in the sand dunes, and through meadows full of buttercups and cows. About half way along the distance to Brora, I came into a bay full of basking seals. They were so still I'd actually gone past them thinking they were rocks, until I heard this strange ghostly barking noise, and stopped to investigate. Through the binoculars I then saw that at least half the rocks were in fact seals! So I retraced my steps and spent an hour or so watching them. They lay on the top of rocks, huge and comically balanced on their sides, looking so uncomfortable. As the tide came in and their rock-top resting places submerged, they heaved themselves onto the sand further up the beach. I was told later they were common grey seals and I needn't have been so careful not to disturb them because they're not worried by human activity. The whole of today's path was beautiful, made especially so because of the brilliance of the light and dark cloud patterns reflected onto the sea.

Brora is a nice wee place and I had some soup in a café and did some food shopping in case there would be no food at the B&B, which is more than a mile outside Brora. I knew I'd got dinner ordered at one of my pre-booked B&Bs but couldn't remember which. Happily it turns out to be here, so I'm going to have lasagne for supper and I'll eat the food I bought today on tomorrow's longer journey to Helmsdale.

Saturday 19 June
Brora - Helmsdale
Had a lovely time last night talking to another 'End to Ender!' This was Tom Isaacs, who set off from John O'Groats only a few days ago and hopes to reach Land's End on September 6. It was great to be with someone else doing the same thing, for the first time. I hardly ever meet another walker, let alone somebody doing the whole works. We exchanged notes and compared equipment and laughed because we had precisely the same photocopied pages of McCloy folded into our maps! He wanted to know about the road ahead, all of it! But he couldn't help me much as he'd come a different route from John O'Groats, over the hills following McCloy. He's doing it in aid of Parkinson's Disease, but it was only this morning that I found out he has the disease himself, so young - only 31, the same age as Michael. He gave me £5 for the LRF and I gave it back to him for Parkinson's Research. We exchanged addresses and left our B&B together to walk the mile back into Brora, where he turned south and I north, into the pouring rain. I hope he saw the seals.

So near the end now, I can't wait to see Berwyn and the kids and to be home again. Also to see the possibility of realising all the plans I've been hatching during the past weeks! The most elaborate (and expensive!) of these are for the proposed Jim garden behind the barn. Planning this has kept me going along many a main road or on days when I wasn't feeling so good. I found I could just switch into those plans and bingo! I'd forget the hard road and its traffic, or the painful toes, aching limbs or whatever, and be away planting a rose trellis, building a wall or working out the levels between barn and bank. A bit like self-hypnosis I suppose.

I'm in the youth hostel here, which is nice, close to the town centre for once, and very basic. The most basic of all in fact, there are only two dormitories, one for women and one for men. Ours has got 16 bunks in it and at the far end there's a washroom with a little row of basins and one lavatory. There's only one shower for the whole hostel, just inside the front door. No drying room even, and because I arrived completely sopping wet, all my things are hanging up on a long string across the dining area. It's quite warm sitting before the gas fire though, and my boots are slowly drying out here too. The warden is an attractive, friendly girl from Glasgow and we've been chatting. Also staying here are two rather odd Australian women who are travelling around, searching out Scotland's spiritual places. Tomorrow they're heading for the Orkneys to see the midsummer night come in over some stones there. They asked me if I'd like to accompany them, but I had to decline. There's also a group of Americans, two couples. All busy cooking. I'd already had fish and chips earlier while I was waiting for the hostel to open. They've got the same 5pm opening hours here as in England, which was a pity on the day when I was so wet (though not as wet as when I arrived in Perth).

The rain was non-stop today but fairly light. Still, walking through even light rain is quite dismal, mainly because you can't stop for a rest or drink or look at the view. There was no view anyway because it was all shrouded in mist and cloud. I walked along the coast for the first few miles, and then had to climb over several fences and the railway-line to get on to the A9 before the beach gave out.

Sunday 20 June
Helmsdale - Berriedale
Poured with rain most of the day and there was a blustery head wind too. Road walking all the way and climbing. Didn't stop except to have a little snack in a lay-by when the rain stopped briefly. High point of the day was when I saw a group of deer, about four adults and a fawn. They were travelling quite fast through the bracken on a steep slope near the road at the Ord of Caithness, very nervous and wary. They didn't see me. It made me think, if there has been one single thing that has sustained me throughout the journey, it has been wild life. Birds in particular. The very minute a bird sings or if, like today, there is a sighting of wild deer, my mood lightens and perspective is restored.

There were steep climbs all day, and the steepest of all was here in Berriedale, where I'm in my pre-booked llama farm B&B. The road plunges down into the village, skips briefly over the river and then soars straight back up the other side. More of a ravine than a valley I suppose. Like a dressmaker's notch. The tiny village huddles at the bottom, looking as if it's long since abandoned any idea of escape. There's a clutch of houses and a post-office; no shop and no sign of life at all. Perhaps they're all asleep. I heaved my way up the hill, foodless, towards the B&B, hoping they'd be able to give me a sandwich or something this evening - a llama sandwich perhaps. Or cold llama and salad.

And yes, they did! Not llama, but cheese sandwich and lovely hot soup. Deirdre and Stan, my friendly hosts, moved up here from Somerset 10 years ago, and they farm llamas, peacocks, ducks, hens and raccoons as a tourist attraction. But it's not an easy life. Most holidaymakers don't go much beyond Inverness, where the Tourist Information people advise tourists 'there's nothing much north of Inverness.' I'd heard this story from several landladies and not surprisingly feelings run high. They are all pretty aggrieved and it's been a bad year so far for tourism. Of course they do get the walkers and cyclists, lots of End to Enders like me, we're two a penny! Talking of which, I was told that a few days ago there were three men doing the journey on penny-farthings, but one of them crashed on the long hill going down into Berriedale and had to be taken to hospital. How awful to do the whole journey and then crash within a couple of days of the end.

It's light nearly the whole night long now, and tomorrow is the longest day.

Monday 21 June
Berriedale - Dunbeath

I got off to a late start because of helping Deirdre with her Market Research survey for Tango drinks. Awful questionnaire, the worst I've seen. She was in a state about the whole thing and wanted to familiarise herself with the questionnaire before she went out on the job. She hates the work anyway but as with the B&B, it supplements the non-existent income from the zoo and keeps the animals afloat, as it were. I finally left there at about midday, but that was fine as I only had about six miles to go. I'd originally intended to walk up Berriedale Water to Braemore and thence to Dunbeath, the pretty way. But because the weather has been so miserable, and because I'm having a day off tomorrow and can explore inland then, I gave in to the temptation of a quick march straight to Dunbeath. There wasn't too much traffic and it finally stopped raining.

Had lunch in the Inver Arms at Dunbeath and then spent an hour or so in the Heritage Centre and watched the video. After that, I was given a private lecture by a research archaeologist working there, who lives locally and is finding out about the origin of Pictish and earlier inscriptions on stones. It was most interesting and something I know nothing about, but once again I'm learning. I've got the hang of the Stuarts and Bonnie Prince Charlie and the Clearances, now for a bit of the early stuff. Dunbeath, indeed the whole of Caithness, is very important archaeologically, apparently even more so than Orkney, where there are so many cairns, burial chambers and standing stones. The Picts were here from the Iron Age until the Norse Vikings arrived about 800-900 AD, and they left very few remains.

Tuesday 22 June
Day off; Dunbeath

Morning: I hope little Dan will be in tonight so I can wish him Happy Birthday. He'll have got the card and the tartan shirt by now. My littlest chap, 25 years old!

This is my last day off and I'm so glad I'm having it here. Dunbeath is going to be for me the very heart of Caithness. It's a lovely village, only marginally spoiled by the A9 running through it on a huge new, elevated bridge. The old bridge, designed by Thos.Telford (who else?) is still there, crossing Dunbeath Water.

The B&B is probably the most picturesque I've stayed in; a white-washed farmhouse with a distinctive heart-shaped ivy tree growing up its end wall, and spectacular views all around. My landlady, Mrs Mary Macdonald, told me how I could walk to the harbour across the cliff-tops behind their farm. So after a leisurely breakfast I did that, and spent ages watching puffins and loads of other seabirds along the craggy sea cliffs. I think there were guillemots, herring gull, other gulls I'm not sure about, cormorants on the lower edges sitting on large grassy nests, and six or seven beautiful puffins. The puffins were young I think, they were just loafing about and appeared to be waiting for something - parents with the dinner probably. There was a large dead seal in the shallows, which I've added to my list of dead animals. It was cold and splattering with rain, but that didn't bother any of us.

Afternoon: The rain cleared away and it's becoming quite warm and balmy. I am now several miles up Dunbeath Strath, by the side of the Water. I've been sitting on a rock watching the dippers. They're lovely birds, I watched one for ages through the binoculars, fine speckledy breast and soft brown colours. Dip, dip, dip goes its tail. It's quite big, twice the size of a wagtail. I know it's definitely a dipper because it's pictured on the information board. This also told me about the Prisoner's Leap, and I climbed up there just now, to gaze at the distance the poor fellow is supposed to have jumped. Having seen the Soldier's Leap at Killiekrankie I felt I had to view the sight of the Prisoner's glory as well. He was also leaping for his life (well, you'd hardly do it otherwise would you!) and his success on reaching the other side was put down to the fact that he was an orphan and had been reared on hinds' milk!

The sun is coming out. This is very like my last lovely day off in Golspie and it's unbelievably lucky considering all the rainy days I've had in the last three weeks. I'm also glad I've got so much spare time, spinning out the walking time so as not to arrive in John O'Groats before Saturday. There are 40 miles to go now and four more days walking. Only three on my own, because with a bit of luck Berwyn and the boys and Tam will reach me at Keiss on Saturday morning to walk the last 10 miles. Michael and Tam will then have walked the first 10 miles and the last! David is coming too, but Dan can't come up because he's only got one day's holiday left before next year. So he's injecting the cat and keeping the home fires burning. The thought of sitting by a big fire in the sitting room is so good, but apparently it's much too hot for that, incredible thought that seems, here in the wintry north of Scotland.

This beautiful place, the birds, the sound of rushing water over stones, and now the warm sun, have all combined to make me feel better again. Melancholy had struck once more during the last couple of days - probably a consequence of the incessant rain. Thank goodness I didn't keep to an idea I'd had at the beginning, to write the history of Jim's 15 weeks in hospital during the equivalent 15 weeks of the walk. Think what I'd be writing now.

But I can never forget that we did have those ten precious days, lasting until three days before he died and beginning with the morning when he woke up and said, or rather, whispered, 'I feel better!' And he did too. He was able to eat again, hungry for the first time in months, his appetite improving so quickly that within a few days we were taking him a whole plateful of roast beef! In the night I lay on the little camp bed in his room listening to the joyful sound of him peeling the wrappers off chocolate bars. I think it was the happiest time of my whole life, despite how he looked (skeletal), how desperately ill he still was, and the long haul ahead with more chemotherapy and the bone marrow transplant essential to his survival. During those ten days he was happy too. He saw all his friends again and made plans, scanning the latest music magazines for the electronic equipment he was going to buy, using the monies he'd received a few weeks earlier from the Football Italia music they'd sold to Television.

We had long talks in the early mornings, during those precious days. Once he clapped his hands to wake me up - there wasn't anything the matter, he just wanted to have a chat! Another time, he asked me, 'Did you ever think I might die?' And when I said, 'Yes,' after only a moment's hesitation because honesty was of such crucial importance throughout the whole of that time, he immediately said, 'Oh, that must have been awful!' His first thought was for me and for all of us. Even though it must have brought home to him the reality of his situation, a verification of what he must have long suspected. He always hated the idea of other people being hurt by anything that he had done or said, however inadvertently. He was so gentle - loving harmony, hating discord. That is why I know we have to try and regain a level of happiness, for his sake. If he's somewhere or if he's nowhere, he's suffered enough without having to carry the weight of our continuing unhappiness on his shoulders as well. And that is also why this walk essentially had to be for fun, me indulging myself for three and a half months. There would have been no point in doing it otherwise. Jim would have had no patience with that, and neither would I.

What will it be like I wonder, when I get home? Can't imagine. I've got so used to living each day as it comes and only having to bother with the idle thoughts that drift through my head, if and when. All the necessities of daily living: planning, talking, jobs (housework, gardening), shopping, socialising, all the things that I haven't had to bother with for three and a half months, will once more have to be accommodated. And after all, nothing has changed. Jim is still not there, nor ever will be. He's not in Stonegate churchyard either, but I'll still go there because it's the most of him that there is.

All I want now is to be home - fire, Socky-lockys, garden, tea in bed, long hot baths. And I shall think back to some of these days - this day - and be so grateful that I've had this journey. Jimmy's and my journey.

But that brings me to another thing I've been thinking about recently. I've already written about the three-fold reasons for the journey, and how the balance in terms of importance has shifted at different times and stages. The fundraising aspect took a back seat fairly swiftly, but the other two reasons have remained constant, fluctuating occasionally so that sometimes the Jim factor would take precedence and sometimes it seemed as though it was all for me. Increasingly, the two have become intertwined: Jim's lap of honour, my little interlude. But now the whole enterprise is coming to an end - he's gone *and* his journey is ended. So a part of me feels totally bereft and I'm wondering what can I do now to keep him by me. It's all very well to talk of his influence always being with us, photos, memories and so on, but there are times when I howl for the want of something more tangible.

Wednesday 23 June
Dunbeath - Lybster

I was sad to leave after two nights in what was probably my best B&B of the whole walk. Everything about it was perfect: my pretty bedroom under the eaves, the farm outside the backdoor, views over the surrounding country, cliff-top fields reaching out to the sea, and Mrs Mary Macdonald herself. She was so very sweet, a typical farmer's wife in some respects, but with an extra quality difficult to define, but made me realise she was a person I would never forget. She and her husband have lived on the farm (owned by the local landowner, not them) all their married lives, and her husband has never been even as far as Inverness! Couldn't bear to leave the animals.

Once again I've had no pack to carry because Mary insisted on driving it to my Lybster B&B. And the weather was marvellous, bright blue sky and no clouds. Even though I stopped for quite a while at the Gunn Museum, I still got here early, and went to have a bite to eat at the Bayview Hotel. Then I proceeded down to the harbour to kill a few more hours before presenting myself at the B&B. Brenda, my landlady tonight, is young, with two children and her husband died of leukaemia last year. I was told this by my previous two landladies, who both know her. She's very nice and busy with the kids' school concert tonight, so I'm having a quiet peaceful time. The last three nights I've had chats all evening, so it's good to be on my own again. Nine o'clock and I'm tucked up in bed. Felt tired all day, had pains in arm/chest again, and still got the tummy upset. Otherwise fine and NEARLY THERE!

I learnt that my relatives the Sinclairs[41] were all from up here in north Caithness. And that Henry Sinclair was probably the very first person to find America! After the Vikings, that is, but long before Columbus. The Sinclair clan chiefs also lived in Dunrobin Castle at one point, before the Sutherland dukes moved in. What's more, it was a Sinclair who first introduced the Cheviot sheep to that area - that did so well that it started the rot of the clearances. Learnt all this in the Gunn Museum; the Sinclairs were the big rivals and enemies of the Gunn clan, whose last outpost on the edge of the barren cliffs at Baobae I visited the other day.

---

41. My great, great grandmother was a Sinclair before her marriage, and her grandfather, James Sinclair, was born in Thurso (in 1744).

Thursday 24 June
Lybster - Wick

Had long chats with Brenda this morning. She's such a sweet person and so brave. It's been really tough for her with her two little daughters to look after in their grief too. She told me that her older daughter, who is probably about 11 or 12 years old, is still very angry, and had bombarded the local minister with questions when he called. He completely failed to answer her questions, and, to his shame, has never been back since. Brenda was taken aback and slightly shocked by the intensity of her daughter's questions, but proud of her all the same for venturing into what she considered the minister's territory.

I didn't like Wick very much, at least, the parts that I saw. Dirty harbour, public squalor, and disaffected youth with nothing to do hang around the town centre in the evening. For the first time in the whole trip I felt slightly wary after I'd got money out of the hole in the wall of the Bank of Scotland, and did a bit of a detour rather than go back the way I'd come with a pile of money in my pocket.

Nearly there, nearly there! I kept scrutinising the horizon ahead to see if I could glimpse the sea in front of me for the first time, but I couldn't. It was a long day's road walk, about 15 miles. Feet, ankles and legs all covered in rash again so it must have been long. Feel better in myself though.

Berwyn, Michael, David and Tam will set off about 5am tomorrow for their long drive up. Can't wait to see them! I hope never to be separated from them for so long again.

Local news: *Reporting Scotland.*

Friday 25 June
Wick - Keiss

Lovely day again and the nine miles here were quite easy. Called in at Caithness Glassworks since I had time on my hands. It was fascinating watching them make the glass, fashioning it into different shapes. I spent ages gawping at them from the visitors' standpoint. I would have bought something there too had there been anything small and pretty, but I couldn't see anything of the finished product that I liked. Why don't they make pretty jewellery for example, coloured glass earrings or pendants? And if there had been a nice chunky little glass or something I'd have bought it for Berwyn. Price no object. Wanted to give him a little something.

Anyway, what has just happened: As I was lounging on the bed in my nice room in the Sinclair Bay Hotel, watching the tennis and drinking tea, the landlord came up to say my son Michael was on the telephone and that they were going to be here earlier than expected! I rushed downstairs with him and there was sweet Mikey's voice on the telephone sounding so happy and excited! They were in Inverness already, in fact, this side of Inverness, and it was only 4.45pm! I could hardly believe it - they must have come terribly fast. But as both Michael and David are insured to drive the car as well for the journey, I dare say they had a hand in the speed of time! So they're going to stay here in the hotel with me, and we'll have an extra night together.

I'm really getting excited now! I'm much more excited to be seeing all of them again than nearly finishing the journey. Today I tried to feel excited about that, or pleased or gratified or something, and just couldn't manage it. I'm sure everyone will want to know how I felt, with the end in sight and so on, but it honestly doesn't feel as if it's anything special. I'll be glad it's finished, glad to go home and more than anything glad to be with Berwyn and all the kids again. Those are my only thoughts.

So they'll be here in about an hour and a half! And we can all have supper here, no more lonely suppers! Last night's supper in Wick was not very nice, though the place was alright, recommended by my landlady and good value for money: three course meal of soup, sirloin steak and pudding all for £4.99, special offer. But the steak had a funny taste to it and I couldn't eat it, either it was a bit off, or it was because my tummy was still a bit wobbly.

Can't believe they'll be here so soon! Fingers crossed.

Saturday 26 June
Keiss - John O'Groats

Last night all that was missing was little Dan, though I did talk to him on the phone. I was so excited when they all arrived that I kept thinking I'd finished the journey, and so one of my first thoughts was, 'I must ring Dan!'

It was wonderful to see them all. I'd seen the car coming over the horizon from my bedroom window and so was waiting by the side of the road when they arrived. And then there was a peculiar moment when nothing seemed to happen. There was a lull, and I thought, 'Why don't they get out of the car?' It can only have been for a split second, but it seemed to last forever. I suppose it was a distortion of time such as you hear people describe when they're about to experience a car crash or similar - moments of danger or high emotion, when 'time stood still.' I've never experienced it before. But they did get out eventually, beaming and smiling, and then we were all kissing and hugging each other in the quiet, dusty road outside the Sinclair Bay Hotel, and I shall never forget it. They thought I looked thin and I thought they looked wonderful! We had a lovely meal together, everybody talking at the same time, and I've no notion of what we ate.

And how lovely to set out all together this morning, me without a care in the world! (Still carrying my pack though, emptied of some of its contents. I wouldn't let them carry it for me on this last day)! Michael, David and Tam accompanied me all the way and Berwyn did a bit of sightseeing in Wick and then parked the car in John O'Groats and walked back out to meet us. It was so good to be walking with them on what I still couldn't quite believe was the last day. It seemed quite normal, though I did feel a bit light-headed and couldn't concentrate at all. It was main road all the way of course but there was hardly any traffic, and we fair skipped along, scrutinising the horizon for our first sight of the sea *ahead*.

At last there it was, the sea in front of us, and the first of many signs saying JOHN O'GROATS. We took lots of pictures, draping ourselves around the signs, and walked the last few hundred yards to The End. It's far nicer here than in Land's End with its theme park and commercial tat. John O'Groats is just a big hotel (the original house of Jan der Groot, and most of which was closed for refurbishment), the sea, and a few small souvenir shops selling lots of postcards. There were some picnic tables outside the hotel and so we made our way there with all the goodies Berwyn had bought in Wick. Another Land's End/John O'Groats walker had arrived about half an hour previously and so we joined forces after a bit and compared notes in an excited, disjointed sort of way. The boys couldn't get over the size of his calf muscles! He was surrounded by his support team, who had arranged for a piper to pipe him in, followed by the presentation of an engraved Caithness glass paperweight, by an official from Caithness District Council. Meanwhile, we were happily popping our own champagne corks and eating sandwiches at the next-door table. Then I, too, was presented with a Caithness glass paperweight by the nice councillor, who hadn't known I'd be there of course, and must have been thanking his lucky stars he had a spare one with him. He even apologised for the fact that it was three years out of date! The family and supporters of the other walker offered me a loan of the piper so that I could have my photo taken with him, and we all milled around talking and laughing in friendly and slightly embarrassed fashion on this unique, never-to-be-repeated occasion. What an extraordinary day! And how happy I am to be going home tomorrow!

Postscript

Nearly two years have elapsed since I returned from the walk and I am astonished by the clarity of my memories. Of course, the very act of writing a diary enhances memory, to say nothing of the refresher course mine has undergone recently as a result of editing the material for this book. But I have been surprised by the number of events, people or scenes that are not mentioned in the diary, but that remain so vividly in my memory I'm amazed I didn't write about them at the time. Some of these unrecorded memories are of quite substantial happenings, but mostly they consist of tiny fragments; fleeting moments too ordinary to take much notice of at the time, but that now furnish a rich seam of reminders, there for the picking. There's the picture of a solitary tractor, for example, ploughing the dark red soil of a field near Pitlochry, followed by a cloud of seagulls. The farmer raises his hand in greeting and it's as if there is only him, the birds and me in the whole world. A more generic memory is of sheepdogs lying silent and inscrutable at the entrance to farms in north Devon, never flicking so much as an ear at my approach. And another (burnished, this one, from frequent picking out of the memory seam) of a straggle of cows, escaped from their field and grazing the much sweeter grass verges, as we all meander together along the evening lane towards Kington.

I remember every B&B, every village I stayed in, every youth hostel. I remember large chunks of Hereford, Shrewsbury, Carlisle and Inverness. And all of Balerno. Pictures spring into my mind of places that were once just names, and I bore my family rigid by the frequency with which I'm able to interject the now dreaded phrase: "Oh! I've been there!"

The memories will fade I know, but the diary remains as a factual reminder of a walk that was everything I expected, and more. It has become an indelible part of my life and I never cease to be grateful that I had the chance to do it.

Coming home was wonderful too. I didn't feel bad, or restless, or unduly upset about Jim all over again. Life returned to normal as quickly as it always does when you return from a holiday.

As a result of the walk, the friends who joined me for a stretch on the way now form the nucleus of a small group who walk every week - through all weathers, and all of us encased in Paramo. We are about to complete the second half of the South Downs Way, and may even diversify into cycling!

The walk was unexpectedly successful financially, too. I didn't set out to make it a sponsored event, mainly because of the boys' sponsored cycle ride completed only the previous summer. So having secured sponsorship from Nikwax, and written the letter to George Michael, I figured that, together with any contributions offered me on the walk, I might be able to raise between £1000 - £2000 for the Leukaemia Research Fund. It was much more than that! Nikwax was incredibly generous, presenting me with a cheque for £2500, five times the amount I expected. This, coupled with George's astonishing donation of £10,000, and the £800 I collected en route, meant that the walk actually raised about £13,300. We were delighted, because it meant that when this sum was added to the previous year's cycle ride monies, and the profits from a memorial concert given for Jim in London, the grand total raised for the Leukaemia Research Fund now exceeded £20,000.

In some ways, the writing of this book has become an extension of the walk. It began with the typing up of my scribbled notebooks, for the family to read if they wished and for my own future use. It was never my intention to publish the contents of the diary. But the typing and the tinkering became irresistibly absorbing, and lead eventually and perhaps inevitably to this book that catalogues my walk experiences in their entirety. With a few changes, it is a faithful copy of the diary as it was written each evening at the end of the day's walk. The changes consist mainly of the elimination of tracts I felt might be either tedious or too sad, and a few additions of an explanatory nature. It is far removed from the slim factual volume I originally envisaged as

I tripped down from Offa's Dyke that April day into the waiting Shropshire countryside. My intention then was to publish a rough description of my route that was turning out so well, so that other people, armed with the appropriate OS maps, would be able to follow some, or all, of my journey. I still hope they will do that, adding their own refinements of course and avoiding some of my pitfalls. I hope at least that they will be encouraged in the endeavour. And if the book is picked up for its diary contents only - why then! I hope they enjoy that too.

June 2001

Lists

Dead Animals

Badgers x 2

Lambs x 8

Hedgehogs; too many to count

Rat x 1

Cats x 5

Pheasants; too many to count

Wren x 1

Rabbits; far too many to count

Magpie x 1

Crows; too many to count

Mole x 1

Hare x 1

Chaffinch x 2

Shrews; too many to count

Sloe worm x 1

Snake x 1

Deer x 3

Bullfinch x 2

Little bird with yellow speckledy breast that I've seen so often x 1

Bluetit x 1

Lizard x 1

Seal x 1

Lapwing x 2

Seagulls; too many to count

Wagtail x 1

Counties	Long Distance Paths	
Cornwall	South West Coastal Path	7 days
Devon	Cheddar Railway Walk	1 day
Somerset	Severn Way	1 day
Gloucestershire	Wye Valley Walk	8 days
Monmouth	Offa's Dyke Path	2 days
Herefordshire	Jack Mytton Way	1 day
Powys	Shropshire Way	2 days
Shropshire	Sandstone Trail	2 days
Cheshire	Cheshire Ring Canal Walk	2 days
Lancashire	Cumbria Way	6 days
Cumbria	Southern Upland Way	1 day
Dumfries & Galloway		
Roxburghshire		
Peebles-shire		
Midlothian		
Fifeshire		
Inverness-shire		
Ross-shire		
Sutherland		
Caithness		
Total 20 counties		

Clothes & Equipment

Backpack	Torch
(Lowe Alpine 60 + 15 capacity)	Camera
Leather boots (Meindl)	Calculator (slim)
Paramo windproof jacket & fleece	Penknife
Paramo trousers	Survival bag
Waterproof jacket	Compass
Light trousers	Maps & map case
Polartec shirts x 2	Map wheelie
(1 long-sleeved, 1 short-sleeved)	Whistle
Light, short-sleeved shirt	Water bottles x 2
Good walking socks x 2	Boot wax
Evening socks x 2	Washing powder
Light shoes	List of addresses
Mackintosh cover for backpack	Notebooks & biros
Stick	Book
Bumbag	Tissues
Daypack	Spectacles
Woolly hat, gloves, scarves x 2	Binoculars
Light windcheater top	Fluorescent armbands
Gaiters	Leukaemia Research Fund
Nightie	papers
Underwear x 2	Medical card
Towel	Youth Hostel membership card
Sponge-bag	RSPB membership card
First-aid bag	Credit card, cheque book, coins
Silver sitting square	Telephone

Milage Totals

	Mileage	Walking days	Average miles per day	Days off
Stage I	224	20	11.2	2
Stage II	219	20	11	0
Stage III	210	19	11	3
Stage IV	237	19	12.5	1
Stage V	186	19	9.8	3
Total	1076	97	11.1	9